"Like most women today, I struggle with feelings of 'too much to do and too little time to do it'! My friend Carolyn Mahaney, along with her daughters, offers practical, biblical advice to help us plan, evaluate, strategize, and make wise choices concerning our time and priorities. As a godly mentor, Carolyn takes us by the hand, points us to God's Word, shares out of her own life experience, and shows us how to apply God's timeless truths to the contemporary challenges we face as women."

Nancy DeMoss Wolgemuth, author; *Revive Our Hearts* radio host

"'We can actually do *all* that God has called us to do . . . and we can do it in a peaceful, joyful manner and get sufficient rest beside.' When I read that, a light flashed on in my soul. Of course! I knew that! Once again Carolyn, Nicole, Kristin, and Janelle have created a book that's fun to read and filled with truth that resonates because it's biblical, practical, and manageable. And lest I start to feel overwhelmed, their husband and dad, C.J., inserts another comforting truth: 'Only God gets his to-do list done each day.'"

Noël Piper, wife, mother, grandmother; author, *Faithful Women and Their Extraordinary God*

"*Shopping for Time* offers a glimpse into the delightful Mahaney household. Through the effective use of a shopping metaphor, the conversational style engages the reader from start to finish. Quotes from carefully selected resources would make for excellent further study. This book offers no simplistic solutions to the perils of superwoman syndrome. Instead, it deliberately leads women to the bedrock of biblical priorities and then suggests real life methods by which to apply them. The wise woman will redeem her time by prayerfully heeding the seasoned advice of Carolyn Mahaney, one of God's choicest servants, and her amazing, godly daughters."

Mary K. Mohler, wife of Dr. Al' President, The Southern Baptist

D1472030

shopping for time

OTHER CROSSWAY TITLES
by Carolyn Mahaney

Girl Talk
Carolyn Mahaney and Nicole Whitacre

Feminine Appeal
Carolyn Mahaney

True Beauty
Carolyn Mahaney and Nicole Whitacre

shopping for time

How to Do It All and NOT Be Overwhelmed

Carolyn Mahaney
Nicole Whitacre
Kristin Chesemore
Janelle Bradshaw

WHEATON, ILLINOIS

ISBN: 978-1-4335-5299-1
ePub ISBN: 978-1-4335-2061-7
PDF ISBN: 978-1-4335-0172-2
Mobipocket ISBN: 978-1-4335-0865-3

Library of Congress Cataloging-in-Publication Data
   Shopping for Time: How to Do It All and NOT Be Overwhelmed
Carolyn Mahaney . . . [et al.].
      p. cm.
   ISBN 13: 978-1-58134-913-9 (tpb)
   ISBN 10: 1-58134-913-0
    1. Christian women—Religious life. I. Mahaney, Carolyn, 1955–
II. Title.
BV4527.S435   2007
248.8'43—dc22   2007008075

Crossway is a publishing ministry of Good News Publishers.

VP		25	24	23	22	21	20	19	18	17	16
13	12	11	10	9	8	7	6	5	4	3	2	1

To
CALY and TORI,
future shoppers of time.

Contents

Introduction

It's one o'clock on a Friday afternoon and the four of us, Mom and daughters, are sitting around Mom's kitchen table. The grandsons and granddaughters have been deposited in various rooms throughout Mom-Mom's house for rest times or naps. And we're enjoying carryout from our favorite Greek restaurant down the street.

It's girl time, for just a little while. And because we're the best of friends, we've been looking forward to this hour at Mom's kitchen table all week long.

Janelle has one eye on her French fries, which are crisping in the oven. Perfectly cooked fries are her idea of gourmet cuisine. Kristin's already gulped down about two gallons of Mom's southern sweet tea. To watch her drink, you'd think she hadn't had a drop of liquid in two days, that girl. Nicole's too busy talking to eat much of her meal. Mom, the steady, dependable one, is placidly enjoying her usual order—a Greek salad with grilled chicken. In the middle of the table, where the centerpiece used to be, is a giant container of feta cheese, which we all take turns dumping on our food. It would sound more polite to say we sprinkle it on our food, but that wouldn't be quite accurate. To be completely honest, you'd have to say we like a little Greek food with our feta cheese.

Each daughter usually comes with her own agenda. Janelle has funny stories to tell and we laugh until we choke on our food (or drink, in Kristin's case). Kristin seems to have an endless supply of heartbreaking tales, and we have to cut her off before we get too depressed. Nicole brings a list of serious issues to discuss, which sound very much like the ones she brought up last week (although she claims they are entirely different).

Mom is the listener and chief advice dispenser. And as fellow pastors' wives and mothers, we daughters have oodles of questions we've been storing up all week. "What do I do when the boys won't share their toys?" "How should I counsel a woman who struggles with condemnation?" "What is one way I can encourage my husband as he juggles his work and school load?"

When one of us asks a question, the rest of us jump in with our opinions—all at the same time. But in the end, we look to Mom, the wise sage-ess (what else do you call a female sage?), for the definitive word.

Today we're talking about the e-mails we receive on our blog (www.girltalk.blogs.com), and specifically this one from a young girl named Kasy:

> Although I'm only seventeen years old and don't yet have the responsibilities of a homemaker, wife, and mother, I'm finding myself very overwhelmed with my current season of life. I am working about five hours a day, three days a week, trying to complete my senior year of high school,

babysitting twice a month, attending a ladies' Bible study at church weekly, etc. And starting this Friday, I'll be adding three Friday nights and one Saturday a month with youth events at church. I've been so overwhelmed, and it's making me miserable.

Overwhelmed. Miserable. Exhausted. We know the feeling well. As wives and mothers with toddlers and teenagers, and husbands who serve as local church pastors, we often feel pulled in five directions at once. We've learned there is no such thing as simply a busy month or a busy year. It's a busy *life*, pure and simple. Around every corner is another potential hospitality, another counseling opportunity, another church meeting, another diaper to change or carpool to run.

But we also have learned from God's Word that it is possible to deal with life's demands without becoming overwhelmed, miserable, and exhausted. We can surmount the numerous responsibilities that threaten to wear us down. More than that, we can actually do *all* that God has called us to do.

"Ha," you laugh. "You've got to be joking! Do it all? You haven't seen my to-do list. It's longer than an unwound roll of toilet paper!"

A fantastic claim, we know. But it's true. We can accomplish everything God has ordained for us to do in this life. (Hint: It's probably not half of what's on your to-do list.) And we can do it in a peaceful, joyful manner and get sufficient rest besides.

But *how*? We've written this book to answer that question—for Kasy and every other seventeen-, twenty-seven-, and fifty-seven-year-old woman who may be overwhelmed, miserable, and exhausted.

So come join us at Mom's kitchen table, won't you? Pull up a chair. Here's the carryout menu. Pick what you like; it's on Mom. We'd love to have you be a part of the conversation as it's bound to be a lively one. Oh, and please pass the feta.

CHAPTER ONE

Shopping for Time

The bargain was simply too good to pass up. Never mind that she was in Florida visiting her mother and that her kitchen pantry was a thousand miles away in Maryland. Mom has never been easily deterred when she's convinced something will serve her family. It was 1979, and as a young homemaker on a meager budget, Starkist tuna fish at twenty-nine cents a can would help stretch her grocery money.

So she ran over to Publix supermarket and snatched up some sixty cans of the white chunk fish in water. (It was probably soon thereafter when grocery stores began imposing limits per offer.) Mentally preparing overstuffed tuna fish sandwiches with chopped pickle, and creamy tuna broccoli casserole, she giddily paid the cashier. Back at Grandma's house, Mom stuffed the precious discs in shoe-toes, between layers of clothing, and alongside her toiletries. Somehow she managed to cram all sixty cans into an already-full suitcase.

And yes, every last can made it safely back to our Aquarius Avenue duplex where we kids and Dad were served a variety of tuna dishes for weeks on end. This probably explains our strong aversion to tuna casserole that persists to this day.

You may chuckle at the idea of a suitcase full of tuna fish, but you won't laugh too loudly. That's because you've probably got your own tuna fish story. And what's more, you're proud of it. We women take our shopping seriously.

We scour the Sunday paper for coupons and sales. We haunt thrift stores. We track down bargains better than a hound dog on a scent. We stalk a falling price as closely as a Wall Street trader follows a promising stock. We've even been known to commit acts of insanity like camping out overnight just to be first in line for a half-price sale or advancing on the shopping mall the day after Thanksgiving.

We're experts in our trade. We know which time of year to shop for what items. We know which supermarket has the best produce and where to find the best deals online. We don't get taken in by anyone, and, like Mom, we never pass up a good deal.

The reality is, however, we don't often manage *the time* God has granted us on this earth with the same intentionality or skill that we bring to shopping. Think for a minute:

- Do you plan ahead to maximize your fruitfulness each day, or do you simply let life happen?
- Do you make choices based on Scripture or on what feels good at the moment?
- Do you strategize to use your talents to bless your family and church, or do you employ them primarily for your own personal fulfillment?
- Do you evaluate every opportunity in light of biblical priorities, or do you do whatever it takes to get ahead?

• Do you consider whom God would have you serve, or do you try to please everyone all the time?

While we constantly—almost unconsciously—plan, evaluate, strategize, and make wise choices when shopping, we often neglect to do so with the most important matters of our lives. We wouldn't dream of going to the grocery store without a shopping list, or buying a car without haggling over the sticker price, or purchasing new shoes without checking the price tag, but we throw away our time as if we had an endless supply.

As a result, we often miss out on the best deals life has to offer and end up paying big time in guilt, anxiety, and a lack of confidence that we're really doing the will of God. More often than not, we're overwhelmed by life's choices and demands. Perhaps most unfortunately, we lack fruitfulness in Christ's kingdom.

But it doesn't have to be like this. We can know—with absolute certainty—that we are doing all God wants us to do. Peace and joy and rest can be an everyday experience. We can live a life worthy of the calling to which we have been called (Eph. 4:1). And we can anticipate that future day when we will hear those words—"Well done, good and faithful servant. . . . Enter into the joy of your master" (Matt. 25:21).

How? *By becoming shoppers of time.* This isn't our bright idea. It comes straight from Scripture. Ephesians 5:15–16 tells us how to live like we shop: "Look carefully then how you walk, not as unwise but as wise, making the best use of the time, because the days are evil."

Look Carefully

Check out the first part of this verse: "Look carefully then how you walk, not as unwise but as wise." It's a sobering command, is it not? It means that we are to walk with the utmost accuracy, with extreme care. The NKJV reads: "See then that you walk circumspectly." To be circumspect means to look around with caution.

We are not to trudge blindly or routinely through our days. We shouldn't just let life happen and try to deal with the results, be what they may. We should not allow one day to flow simply into the next, being concerned only with the present moment. No, we must look around. We must develop keen eyes. We must examine our lives. We must evaluate our present manner of living and consider how to prepare for the future. We must walk circumspectly through each and every day.

After all, we wouldn't dream of sauntering through a clothing store with our eyes closed, picking up whatever we touch, placing it on the counter, and hoping it would turn into a wardrobe. No, we carefully walk through the store with our eyes wide open. We consider style. We study the price tag. We evaluate quality.

This verse in Ephesians tells us to live the way we shop—carefully. It means we look *backward* and ponder our life thus far so that we might avoid past errors and repeat former victories. It necessitates that we look *forward* and not embark upon a course (whether short or long) until we've considered where it will lead. It requires us to take an honest look *inside* and question our motives, our reasons for the choices that we make. It means we look *around* and take stock of our present fruitfulness. It entails looking *beside* us for critique, help, and wisdom from fellow believers. Most importantly, it means we look *up* and seek guidance from God's Word. This is how to be intentional, purposeful, and, as this verse says, *wise* in the way we walk.

Oh, and did you notice that there are only two kinds of

women mentioned here—the wise and the unwise? With its usual bluntness, Scripture makes it clear that there is no third option. We are either wise or unwise. Smart or foolish. And of course, none of us wants to be a fool! Fortunately, the next part of this verse tells us how to avoid this fate: by *making the best use of the time.*

Making the Best Use of the Time

This phrase, "making the best," means to "buy up, rescue from loss, or improve" the use of time. It is a metaphor taken from the merchants and traders of the ancient Near East, who aggressively pursued the best deals when they would buy, sell, or trade. (We told you this idea of "shopping for time" comes straight from Scripture!)

Actually, this brings to mind another of Mom's shopping stories. As you know, the time right after Christmas is the peak of bargain-hunting season. The stores are plastered with large, inviting "Half-Price Sale!" and "75 Percent Off!" signs, and you rarely find something at full price. Well, one extra-busy winter Mom missed those all-important, after-Christmas sales. And when the following Christmas rolled around, she realized the serious consequences of not buying up when the buying was good.

Have you ever bought Christmas wrapping paper at the beginning of December? It costs something like ten dollars a yard, which is what Mom ended up spending. Some of her gifts weren't worth the paper they were covered in! It was painful. So you know where she was the morning after Christmas that year. Yep, she was buying up all the half-price wrapping paper she could get her hands on. And some early Christmas gifts to boot!

That's the idea of this verse in Ephesians. We're to approach life the same way we go after bargains. We need to discern the best opportunities life has to offer. Then we must seize these opportunities and make them our highest priorities. Every day presents us with countless options for how to spend our time. However, only some are truly great deals. Only a few things are really important.

Our job is to figure out what these prime deals are—these key opportunities—and devote all our time and energy to them. This means choosing *not* to do a thousand other things. It means saying no to a lot of enticing options. Here's where it gets tricky. Obviously, we don't want the "bad deals" to keep us from what is truly valuable. We don't want sinful pursuits to deter us from what is God glorifying. But, it's often the good things such as a ministry opportunity, a relational pursuit, a money-making venture, a leisure activity, or a hobby that hinder us from making the *best* choices. It's frequently these good things that distract us from the best things.

So how do we learn to spot the best deals and ignore the bad ones? What are the secrets to discovering life's most excellent bargains? In the following chapters, we will discuss how to become savvy shoppers of time. But first, there is one fundamental principle we must understand.

A Time for Every Season

Think back five years ago. Wasn't your life different from the way it is now? Maybe you weren't even a Christian at that time. Perhaps you have since gotten married or graduated or changed jobs or moved to a new place or had a baby (or two or more!). You may have experienced a life-altering tragedy or a surprising success.

Even if you don't feel as if your life is dramatically different, change has occurred, however imperceptibly. You've probably walked through relational changes, experienced physical changes, learned new skills, or developed new interests. Most significantly, if you are a believer, Christ has been conforming you to his image. Undoubtedly your life is different from the way it was five years ago. And the same will be true five years from now. That's because *our lives are made up of changing seasons.*

It tells us so in Ecclesiastes: "For everything there is a season, and a time for every matter under heaven" (3:1). This biblical passage goes on to list fourteen couplets that cover the range of human activity. There is "a time to be born, and a time to die; . . . a time to break down, and a time to build up; a time to weep, and a time to laugh; a time to mourn, and a time to dance; . . . a time to keep silence, and a time to speak" (3:2–7). For everything there is a season. For everything there is a time.

So it is with us as women. Our lives are never static or stationary. New seasons keep rolling in—each with its own unique joys and challenges. In fact, just about the time we adjust to our present season, it's time to make way for a new one!

A woman may pass through many seasons in her lifetime. Here are a few:

- Childhood
- Adolescence
- Singleness
- Marriage
- Childbearing
- Mothering preschool children
- Mothering school-aged children
- Mothering teenaged children
- Empty-nesting

- Menopause
- Caregiving to elderly parent(s)
- Grandmothering
- Widowhood

This is not an exhaustive list. There may be additional seasons you will experience and ones you will never pass through. For example, certain women may remain single throughout their lifetime, and not every woman will experience widowhood.

But we must understand the reality of our changing seasons if we want to "look carefully how we walk" and "make the best use of our time," for the best deals vary from season to season. Last year's great bargain might be this year's foolish purchase.

And while we must walk with open eyes and make wise choices in each season, our comfort is this—God orders the seasons of our lives. Even the most difficult ones.

What God Chooses

When young, blond, sweet-as-they-come Cindy caught Bill's eye, she thought it was the beginning of happily ever after. Cindy reveled in her role as wife and homemaker. She enjoyed cooking and decorating. She loved hanging out, playing games, and laughing with her husband. And she looked forward to what she assumed would be the next season of her life: motherhood.

But the season of motherhood never came for Cindy. It was many years before she realized that it probably never would. Soon after they were married, Bill began suffering severe and debilitating fatigue, weakness, and headaches. After a while he could no longer work. Cindy—this woman who wanted nothing more than to be at home—became the sole breadwinner.

Years of doctors, experimental treatments, and special diets availed nothing. Bill only got worse—so sick that he often was unable to leave the house. Finally, Bill and Cindy were forced to move from the church and friends they loved so that they could live in a location that offered a better quality of life for Bill. Gradually, Cindy realized that they would never have a family. This was not the life she had planned. It wasn't what she wanted. She felt stuck in a season that wouldn't end.

Like Cindy, none of us would choose "a time to weep," or "a time to mourn," or a time of sickness—a *life*time of sickness. This isn't what Cindy chose. But it's what God chose for Cindy. Here, inside this truth, Cindy found joy.

No, Bill didn't get better. She didn't become a mother. She still lived far away from dear friends. Yet she came to realize that this life—one she hadn't planned for herself—was the very life God had planned for her. God had designed this long, unexpected, unwelcome season so that Cindy could best glorify him. He had allowed this trial so that he could show his goodness and mercy to Cindy in totally unexpected ways. Cindy found joy when she came to rest in the truth that God orders our seasons.

If you were to meet Cindy, her joy would be immediately obvious. It's a deep joy, infused with peace. And it displays itself in a genuine care for others and continual expressions of gratefulness to God. To be around Cindy is to catch a glimpse of the love and goodness of Christ. Cindy isn't just surviving. She's truly thriving, growing, and rejoicing in the season God has ordained.

Scripture provides ample evidence that God sets the boundaries for each season. God determines when one closes and a new one begins. He is in complete charge and sovereignly rules over every season of our lives. And his purpose for our lives in each season ultimately cannot be frustrated.

Proverbs 16:9 declares, "The heart of man plans his way, but the LORD establishes his steps." Nebuchadnezzar said about God, "All the inhabitants of the earth are accounted as nothing, and he does according to his will among the host of heaven and among the inhabitants of the earth; and none can stay his hand or say to him, 'What have you done?'" (Dan. 4:35). The prophet Jeremiah professed, "I know, O LORD, that the way of man is not in himself, that it is not in man who walks to direct his steps" (Jer. 10:23).

All too often, we arrogantly think we are in charge. We imagine that we're planning and deciding our life's course. Who are we kidding? We need to humble ourselves and acknowledge, "God, you are in charge. And I humbly accept your plan for the changing seasons of my life."

We can trust this God who is in charge because we know his purposes are always directed for his glory and our good (Rom. 8:28). As author Elisabeth Elliot insists, "Everything that happens to you has come through the hedge of His love."[1]

What comfort and rest this brings to our hearts! As we seek to make the best use of time in every season, we can be confident that God's divine wisdom and perfect love direct his purposes in our lives.

Because the Days Are Evil

So why is it so important to become wise shoppers of time in every season? Ephesians 5:16 gives the answer: "Because the days are evil." We know this truth all too well. We only have to pick up a newspaper or turn on cable news to hear about the evil swirling around us. Every day we relate to a world full of sinners, each with their own unique temptations. Not to mention the reality of Satan's attacks. But in truth we need look no further than our very own hearts wherein sin still wages war. We live in a fallen world.

In fact, Matthew 6 reminds us that *each day* brings its own set of troubles. We are continually exposed to evil. Therefore, it is imperative that we choose only the best opportunities each season has to offer, because we never know what trouble is waiting for us today—or tomorrow.

We're not trying to depress you or, worse yet, awaken fear. For while evil is a reality we must not ignore, it is not more powerful than our Savior. Jesus himself confirmed, "In the world you will have tribulation." However, he went on to say, "But take heart; I have overcome the world" (John 16:33).

Through our Savior's death and resurrection, sin's rule in our hearts has been conquered, and Satan has been crushed under Christ's heel. Nothing in this world is out of his sovereign control. What's more, God uses even the evil in our lives for his glory and our good. So the reality of evil is not to produce fear but rather to inspire carefulness. It is to provoke us to live wisely—to encourage us to buy up the best deals in each and every season.

Five Tips

Because the days are evil, we must become prudent, circumspect shoppers of time. We can't afford to browse through life "just looking." This is serious business with eternal repercussions. That's why in the following chapters, we want to offer five tips for becoming wise shoppers of time:

1) Rise early.
2) Sit still.

3) Sit and plan.
4) Consider people.
5) Plan to depend.

These tips are not our attempt at Christian-coated time management principles. Rather, they are biblical, life-tested practices we trust will encourage and assist you to bring glory to the Savior through every season of your life. So will you come shopping for time with us? We hope you'll find some deals that are simply too good to pass up.

CHAPTER TWO

The First Tip: Rise Early

(Joining the 5 AM Club)

The daughter of Necessity, The 5 AM Club, was born several years ago. At first, she was not well loved. To be honest, she was absolutely loathed. And yet, the longer she lives, the more esteemed she becomes.

The 5 AM Club began when Mom was writing her first book, *Feminine Appeal*. The only way to meet her deadline was to wake up at the insanely early hour of 4:00 AM. Then, when she and Nicole were writing *Girl Talk*, Nicole reluctantly joined her. After the books were off to press, Mom realized that she could extract other significant benefits from those early morning hours, and so The 5 AM Club came to be.

Mom is the founder, chairman of the board, and secretary. Without her, there is no club. She soon convinced five of her family members to join—the three of us girls and two of her sons-in-law (we won't reveal the names of the holdouts!).

The 5 AM Club is still extremely unpopular between about 5:00 and 6:00 each morning; however, it is much appreciated every hour after that. Here is the basic routine: Mom wakes up, pours her coffee, and then places phone calls to the Bradshaw, Chesemore, and Whitacre homes. We all answer in our groggy voices, "Thanks, Mom," and then roll out of bed. For the record: second to Mom, Janelle is the most consistent member of the club. This should give women around the world hope for rising early, because until this past year Janelle would have been the champion sleeper of our family. If Janelle can do it, anyone can.

For a long time The 5 AM Club was merely a Mahaney family club. Then last year we posted the idea on our blog, *girltalk*. Soon, single women, teenage girls, moms—young and old—and even a few men were signing up to join The 5 AM Club. Actually, small groups around the country and the world began to form 5:30 clubs or 6:15 clubs. We'll introduce you to some of our members throughout this chapter.

We know that The 5 AM Club probably sounds like one of the crazier, more unappealing clubs you've heard of. It probably ranks somewhere between the Cold Shower Club and the Eat More Beets Society. However, The 5 AM Club is actually the first of our five indispensable shopping-for-time tips. And while we understand you might be a bit skeptical, stick with us. We took a risk in putting this tip out in front, but we're hopeful you'll be clamoring to join The 5 AM Club really soon!

First, a disclaimer: the point of this chapter is *not* that really godly women get up at 5 AM. Nowhere in the Bible will you find such a principle. Therefore, nowhere in this book do we make that claim. The goal of The 5 AM Club is simply to promote the benefits of rising early—both for your spiritual life and for the good of your family. *Early*, though, will look different for every woman reading this book. We just call it The 5 AM Club because this is what time we try to roll out of bed. And besides, we thought it sounded nifty.

Radical Measures

The reason The 5 AM Club, or rising early, is the first essential tip for becoming a savvy time shopper is that the second shopping tip—sitting at Jesus's feet—is the most important. And implementing the first tip is often the only way to make the second possible.

To explain what we mean, let us introduce you to a faithful member of The 5 AM Club, a wife and mother named Julie. See if you can relate to her experience:

When my sons were three years and nine months old, I reached a point of desperation. I was exhausted all the time, often getting up in the middle of the night to care for one or both boys. My morning wake-up time happened only when the boys were no longer quiet in their beds. At best, my passion for Christ was lukewarm. I was not enjoying the Holy Spirit's presence on a day-to-day basis in my own home. Sinful attitudes such as anger and judgmentalism were at an all-time high, and my desire to fight sin was weak. I was not quick to humbly receive my husband's counsel. I was not pursuing biblical fellowship. I felt isolated and alone. I had lost perspective on what my priorities were. In short, I was in emergency mode, and my time alone with the Lord was not in its proper place. Always so much to do—and never enough time to stop and give attention to my soul.

In emergency mode. So much to do. No time for the Lord. Desperate. Alone. No doubt every woman—whether you are a mom, a student, or a businesswoman—can identify. We all want to be consistent to meet with God. And yet it can seem impossible to find a slot in the schedule that we can maintain. So instead we often continue for long periods of time—weeks and even months—convinced there is no alternative.

"When my kids start school, then I'll be able to have steady quiet times again," we tell ourselves. "As soon as I graduate from college and get a job with regular hours, then I'll make the spiritual disciplines a priority," we promise a concerned friend. "This project at work will only last a few more months—then I'll meet with the Lord again," we dismiss our nagging conscience. But one busy season invariably gives way to a busier one. The spiritual disciplines gather more dust at the back of our priorities shelf. Our souls wither and our faith grows dim.

Dramatic action is needed. Enter The 5 AM Club. For many of us, the only cure for our starving souls is to wake up early—or at least earlier than we currently do. It's often the only way we can secure a consistent quiet time to meet with God.

If you have children, you know that the expression "quiet time" after they are awake is something of a misnomer. Or if you work at a job or attend school, being on time is usually non-negotiable. Waking up late means your morning devotions are probably the first to go. Here's Julie again:

> I knew I needed to wake up earlier, but I kept telling myself that I'd never be able to do it. I dreaded the thought of failing yet again. Then it occurred to me that I made time for other things I considered important such as grocery

shopping, showering, doing my makeup, eating, date night with my husband, spending time with friends. Was my love for God truly my highest priority? The realization: My daily schedule was not reflective of a heart set on seeking God first. I needed to take radical measures. If I was going to have consistent and quality time with the Lord, it would need to happen before the rest of the family was up and before the day was rolling. If I waited until the boys always slept through the night or until everything was ideal, it would never happen.

So consider what radical measures *you* need to take. It might just begin with The 5 AM Club.

Why Morning?

"But why do I have to get up early to meet with God?" you ask. "What's wrong with the afternoon or the evening?" Nothing. There is no law in the Bible that dictates when to have a quiet time. In fact, we are to meditate on God's Word day and night! However, there *is* biblical encouragement for rising early to seek the Savior.

Consider the psalmist who directs his prayer to the Lord *in the morning* and then watches for the answer (Ps. 5:3). The Proverbs 31 woman is famous for rising "while it is yet night" to provide food for her family. (We'll consider the ways rising early serves our families later in this chapter.) Finally, and most notably, Jesus himself rose early to pray. Mark 1:35 records, "Rising very early in the morning, while it was still dark, [Jesus] departed and went out to a desolate place, and there he prayed."

Referring to Bible reading and prayer, author John Piper offers this advice:

I earnestly recommend that it be in the early morning, unless there are some extenuating circumstances. Entering the day without a serious meeting with God, over his Word and in prayer, is like entering the battle without tending to your weapons. The human heart does not replenish itself with sleep. The body does, but not the heart. . . . We replenish our hearts not with sleep, but with the Word of God and prayer.[2]

Compelling logic, is it not? We don't want to head unprepared into the daily fray. By rising early we can secure much-needed refreshment for our souls.

Early Benefits

The consequences of a lackluster spiritual life and the advantages of rising early to seek God finally motivated our friend Julie to take action. She began having her husband nudge her awake *and* having a friend call her:

Here we are, three years later, and I'm still waking up early—which for me is quite a miracle. I've never once regretted the days I've risen early. The boys are now five and three, and I am still aware of my desperate state, yet more aware of God's grace. Having my early morning time with the Lord doesn't eliminate my sin or guarantee the day will go as I have planned. But having received fresh perspective and vision, the day starts more peacefully. I now have a much richer understanding of the gospel of grace that transforms me, and I love Christ Jesus more today than ever before.

What a transformation! From desperate to dependent, from sporadic to consistent, from anger and anxiety to peace and perspective, from lukewarm affections to growing love for

Christ—only because, by the grace of God, she applied this valuable tip of rising early.

The 5 AM Club is not only for harried moms. Listen to this testimonial from Jessica on The 5 AM Club as it relates to her and some friends, all college students:

> As a graduate student I am very aware of sleep—the need, desire, and idol it can and often does become during the semester. After reading your post on The 5 AM Club, the Lord opened my eyes to see how beneficial it is for my soul to get up early and read my Bible. I live with four other girls, and we decided to institute our own club for the purpose of change and growth. We formed the 6 AM Club. (We decided we didn't have enough to do if we got up at 5:00, and 6:00 seemed insanely early to us as it is.) We all check on each other to make sure we are awake and then proceed to our family room to do our devotions.
>
> Not only have we, the girls in my house, been transformed with a desire to get up early and start our day off with the Word, but other girls from our campus ministry now have the same desire. When my roommates and I get up, we make about three phone calls to hold other girls accountable. We are hoping that the idea of being disciplined in the morning spreads like wildfire. If it does, I think our lives will be transformed in a way that would make us more dependent on the Word of God with hearts fixated on the cross. So, thanks for your blog post on The 5 AM Club. It has planted a greater thirst for the Word in our souls.

"More dependent on the Word of God with hearts fixated on the cross"—what better incentive is there to wake up early?

Now, remember, we're not saying you must rise early in order to grow in your passion for Christ. Maybe your college classes don't start until 11:00 AM, and you can awake at 8:00

and seek the Lord without distraction. Maybe your children are grown and you are able to have a quiet time after your husband leaves for work. And rising early may not be realistic for moms with young children who still get up at night. You are already a part of The Midnight Club and The 3 AM Club, aren't you? No mother of an infant should be condemned by our thoughts in this chapter. Rather, we hope that you know the Lord's pleasure in your sacrificial care for your little one. For you, The 5 AM Club is an idea to consider in the future. However, for many of us, this kind of radical action is necessary. And maybe even long overdue.

For Our Families

Hands down, the most important reason to rise early is to make meeting with God a priority. Secondarily, however, this practice has great potential to serve your family. Wives and mothers, here's a question for you: Does your husband or children have to wake you up each morning in order to meet their needs because you aren't ready to care for them when they arise?

As we mentioned earlier, the Proverbs 31 woman rose extremely early to provide food for her family. Thankfully for us, we don't have to wake up in time to grind wheat and make homemade bread for breakfast! We can pop a frozen waffle in the toaster and the coffeemaker can brew automatically at whatever time we choose. We have it easy.

But modern conveniences aside, think about your family's needs for a moment. Would it bless your husband to have you cook a hot breakfast or say a cheerful good-bye before he leaves for work? Or would your children's morning schedule run more smoothly if you were one step ahead instead of rushing around?

One woman discovered that rising early meant more to her husband than she might have guessed:

God had been tugging at my heart for a while about what time I get up in the morning. I am married to an early bird and I have always resented this trait in him. Getting up before my husband means waking up before 5:30—something that I have really resisted. After reading about The 5 AM Club on your blog yesterday, I knew that I could avoid it no longer. So this morning the alarm went off at 5:20, and I got up. I was awake and available to greet my husband and help get him off to work.

As my husband was leaving, he expressed his gratitude that I had gotten up early. He was thankful, he said, because it showed him where my heart is. If simply serving him this way speaks so loudly about my care for him, I am sorry to have not done it sooner. More importantly, it was a blessing to have that extended time with the Lord.

Thank you for "speaking the truth in love" and helping me to serve my family more effectively. I am praying for God's grace to become a regular member of the club.

This man was grateful for his wife's company in the early morning hours. But look, we realize that for many husbands this may not be important at all. In fact, your husband may prefer you to be wide awake when he arrives home from the office late at night. Or you might have teenagers who are eager to talk only after 10:00 PM, and you don't want to miss those significant conversations.

Obviously, every marriage and family has different dynamics and needs, and changing seasons often require schedule adjustments. That's why it's important to state, again, that The 5 AM Club is founded on principle rather than practice. The question isn't, "How early do you get up in the morning?"

but, "Does your daily schedule reflect your priorities: seeking God at the outset of the day, romancing your husband, and serving your family?" The purpose of getting up early is to make the most important priorities most important. You may not have to get up at 5 AM to do that (We can see it now: 6:30 clubs popping up everywhere!). But consider whether your schedule is truly serving your priorities.

I'm Not a Morning Person

Okay, maybe you're cautiously intrigued. But you're also thinking, "I'm just not a morning person! I've tried before, and I simply can't get up early!" Neither is Janelle a natural morning person, and yet, as we told you previously, she has become a gold-star member of The 5 AM Club. Miracles do happen.

Really, though, it doesn't take a miracle. It requires discipline exercised in reliance upon God's grace. And it might help if we dispel the myth of the morning person—because there is no such thing!

Let's say you live on the East Coast of North America, as we do, and you decide to travel halfway around the world to Bangkok, Thailand. There, it is 3:00 in the afternoon when it is 3:00 in the morning back at home. Would you spend every day in bed because you're not a morning person? Of course not! It would be difficult at first, but you would train your body to adjust. Now, we're certainly not sleep experts, but it's common sense—our sleep pattern conforms to whatever schedule we adopt. If we are not morning people, then chances are we're simply on a night owl's schedule. Martha Peace has some frank words for women who think they are not morning people:

I have heard of women who pride themselves on being "night people." That means they have trouble getting up in the mornings because they come alive at night. They may stay up till all hours reading, watching television, or pursuing some sort of interest. The next morning they are too tired to get up and care for their family. . . . These women are not "night people." They are lazy and selfish. Who would not rather stay up late to do whatever they please and sleep late the next day?

Once a young wife begins getting up earlier than her children and her husband, she will cease to be a "night person." She will be tired at night and go to bed at a reasonable hour so she will be there to serve her family the next morning.[3]

Guilty as charged! We've been those lazy and selfish women—and continue to battle that temptation. Yet each of us can testify that our early morning time is often more profitably spent than our late-night hours.

Now, granted, this isn't true for everyone. C.J. (Dad) has a friend who does his best work between 11:00 PM and 3:00 AM. What's important is to consider how God would have you make the best use of your time.

5 AM Club Hints

We hope by now that many of you are lining up to join The 5 AM Club! Along with your membership certificate (which you'll have to imagine or create for yourself) we want to offer the following suggestions for successful participation. This is Mom's super-secret-six-point strategy for waking up early, and her sleep-loving children can testify that it works:

1. Place your alarm clock in a strategic location, preferably on the other side of the room from your bed.
2. Set your alarm for the same time every day.
3. Never, never, never hit the snooze button or lie back down to catch a few more winks. The second your alarm goes off is the most critical moment in getting up early.
4. Proceed directly to the coffee pot or caffeinated drink of choice.
5. Be prepared to feel absolutely miserable for about ten to fifteen minutes. But the misery soon turns into pure gladness as you experience the delight of meeting with God and reap the benefits the rest of the day. Fifteen minutes of misery is certainly worth fifteen-plus hours of peace and productivity.
6. Remember that our bodies eventually respond to a standard wake-up time. In other words, it gets easier.

There you have it—The 5 AM Club—our first and primo tip for becoming an effective shopper of time. When we rise early, we can walk carefully and make the best use of our time for the good of our souls and the service of our families. So do you want to join our crazy club? Try it for a week or two, and if it doesn't work for you, well, at least there wasn't a membership fee.

CHAPTER THREE

The Second Tip: Sit Still

(Sitting at Jesus's Feet)

When Kristin's three energetic boys visit Mom-Mom's house, they burst in the door—all smiles and yells—and run several laps around her kitchen, hallway, and sitting rooms before coming to a stop (but only for a moment) in front of the jelly bean jar. Candy in fists, they're off again.

In fact, wherever they are—at home, church, or in the store—Andrew, Liam, and Owen are one big happy bundle of constantly moving arms and legs. They jump up and down, wrestle incessantly, and run in circles if there is nothing better to do. Sitting still—not exactly their forte.

So, in an effort to teach them this refined art, Kristin recently instituted "No Moving, No Talking, No Touching (oh, and No Silly Faces) Time." For fifteen minutes or more each day, the boys must sit on the couch with feet forward, folded hands in laps, and of course, no moving, talking, touching (or silly faces!) while Kristin reads to them. You can see the tension in their little bodies, which explodes the minute the kitchen timer rings, and they bound off to one of their favorite activities such as climbing a tree, sword fighting, or kicking the soccer ball. Sitting still is hard work for little boys.

It's not easy for us women either. We're doers, not sitters, by nature. We awake each morning, our minds whirling with all we want to accomplish that day. We bound off to complete these urgent tasks. But we must *sit* before we *do*. In order to effectively shop for time, we must first sit—sit at Jesus's feet.

Of course, you know where we are going with this, don't you? To the biblical town of Bethany and those legendary sisters, Mary and Martha. It's a familiar story, maybe so familiar that we've lost the point:

> Now as they went on their way, Jesus entered a village. And a woman named Martha welcomed him into her house. And she had a sister called Mary, who sat at the Lord's feet and listened to his teaching. But Martha was distracted with much serving. And she went up to him and said, "Lord, do you not care that my sister has left me to serve alone? Tell her then to help me." But the Lord answered her, "Martha, Martha, you are anxious and troubled about many things, but one thing is necessary. Mary has chosen the good portion, which will not be taken away from her." (Luke 10:38–42)

Did you notice the pearl of shopping-for-time wisdom nestled in these verses? Here our Savior unveils the best bargain life has to offer, bar none. "One thing is necessary," he proclaims, "the good portion, which will not be taken away." What is this deal of all deals? Sitting at Jesus's feet and listening to his teaching.

The key to becoming a successful shopper of time is to make our first priority that of seeking God through his Word and prayer. No extra hour of sleep, no "urgent" task we must complete, no service we can do for others is half as good a bargain as this one. In fact, notice it's the "urgent" tasks that distracted Martha from the prize deal in front of her and left her "troubled about many things." C. S. Lewis describes our Martha problem and the solution this way:

> It comes the very moment you wake up each morning. All your wishes and hopes for the day rush at you like wild animals. And the first job each morning consists simply in shoving them all back; in listening to that other voice, taking that other point of view, letting that other, larger, stronger, quieter life come flowing in.[4]

We open our eyes, and the demands of the day come rushing at us like wild animals, don't they? That's why it's ideal to sit and listen at the *outset* of our day—à la The 5 am Club. We must first listen to that other voice, as Mary did. We must first commune with God. For we want his Word—not our demands and desires—to dictate how we use our time.

Not Alone

What happens when we sit at Jesus's feet and listen to his voice? First, pause a moment and consider the stunning implication of this question. Because of his death on the cross for our sins, we have the privilege to sit at the feet of the Wonderful Counselor, Mighty God, Everlasting Father, and Prince of Peace and to listen to him (Isa. 9:6). What marvelous access!

As if it weren't enough to simply bask in his presence, it is here that we receive grace to make the best use of our time. When we seek God through his Word and prayer, we glean *wisdom* for walking carefully. We obtain *guidance* for daily decisions. We find *peace* in the midst of life's whirlwind. We are infused with *strength* to complete our tasks.

Wisdom. Guidance. Peace. Strength. We can't successfully shop for time without them. And we'll only find these essentials by sitting at Jesus's feet. We certainly can't manufacture them on our own. As Jesus plainly puts it in John 15:5, "Apart from me you can do nothing."

One young woman, Abby, learned that there is no substitute for the grace she receives sitting at our Savior's feet:

> I've always struggled with wanting too much sleep. In fact, I often used to sacrifice my personal time with the Lord in the morning so I could sleep longer. Once I had children, my quiet times became even more inconsistent. Not having a set time or a plan to meet with God was hindering my growth and love for the Savior. I was becoming very self-sufficient, trying to live the Christian life without God's grace as my means to obey. Let me just say that it was not fun, and I was constantly failing and feeling condemned. It was a horrible way to live and it was not what God wanted for me.
>
> The Holy Spirit began to convict me and show me that by neglecting to spend time with the Lord on a daily basis, I was becoming dull to spiritual things and adopting a very worldly mindset. By God's grace, I began to get up each morning and spend time reading his Word and praying. My life has been changed ever since. By the power of the Holy Spirit, I have been able to say no to sin, and he has

given me faith for growth in godliness. He has used his Word to convict and encourage me each day. The Lord has made himself greater in my eyes and given me a deeper understanding of his love than ever before. By his grace, I hope I never let another day go by without spending time with my Lord. Not because I want to earn favor from God, but because I need him so much and recognize that only he is truly my sufficiency and my joy.

Scripture is clear about our need for God, as Abby's experience, and indeed our own, consistently bears out. However, our default is still to try and go it alone, despite past consequences. Our daily temptation is to bypass the good portion that Mary chose in favor of our own resources.

We think that we can effectively manage our time, walk carefully, and flawlessly pick life's best deals, independent of sitting at the Savior's feet. We're like a little child who wants someone to watch him create a masterpiece or conquer an endeavor. "Look at me," he'll say, "I can do this *all by myself!*"

It's cute when children assume they can create or accomplish something all by themselves. However, it is altogether different and more serious if we conclude that we can grow in godliness, conquer sin, or spend our time wisely all by ourselves. That's why we must seek God each and every day. If nothing else, sitting at Jesus's feet says to God: "I need you!" It expresses—whether or not we feel it's true—that we know we can't shop for time on our own.

Conversely, choosing *not* to sit at Jesus's feet makes a statement. It says to the Lord, "I can do it without you. I don't need to read your Word or pray or listen to your voice. I am competent all by myself, thank you very much." These are frighteningly arrogant words we're saying, if not with our mouth then with our heart.

Another young mom, Emma, came to realize what her heart was saying when she neglected to meet with God:

Before my son was born, I was faithful to spend time with the Lord in the morning. After his birth, I found myself battling to find a time that would work—where I could sit down, uninterrupted, well rested, with my baby fast asleep in his crib. As I woke up each morning, I was faced with many temptations to do things around the home. I wanted to tidy our apartment, start the laundry, catch up on e-mail, or simply go back to sleep. These things were getting in the way of my time with the Lord.

As a result of not consistently meeting with God, I began to rely on my own schedule and strength to get through the day. When I woke up each morning and failed to prioritize my day to meet with God, when I opened the Bible only when it was most convenient for me, I was making a statement about God. The statement was simply: "I don't need you. I can get by on my own strength." However, my strength was not sufficient! I needed to depend upon the Lord! I needed a consistent time with him so that I could receive his grace.

After much conviction and prayer, I repented of my self-sufficiency. God gave me a renewed desire to spend time with him and a plan for my quiet time that would help me stay consistent. Looking back over this past year, I have seen the Lord's grace so evident in my life. God has allowed me to see the gospel more clearly and apply his Word to my life. As a result, I have come to love and know him more. My time with him is the best part of my day. It reminds me that I am in need of a Savior, whose strength is sufficient for me, and whose grace is available to me.

Like Emma, let's renounce self-sufficiency and begin each day sitting at the feet of our Savior. Please don't assume that because you're not a mom with young children, it's fine for you to meet with God sporadically. All of us—teenagers, singles, married women, grandmothers—need to choose the best portion along with Mary and Abby and Emma. Let's not wait another day to receive God's sufficient strength and abundant grace—that we might look carefully how we walk, making the best use of our time.

How About You?

Perhaps you have been sitting faithfully at the Lord's feet for many years; you have a regular plan for reading God's Word, and you are diligent to pray. For you, this chapter may simply be an encouragement to keep it up. But maybe your times with the Lord have been spotty. And when you do meet with God, you lack direction. You open your Bible and use the point-and-shoot method to decide what to read that day. You are often frustrated by your lackluster prayer life.

If that describes you, you're not alone! We've been there, as have many other women. But we don't want you to stay there. We don't want you to miss out on the abundant blessings that come from day-by-day sitting and listening at God's feet. If consistency is your problem, The 5 AM Club may be your ticket. Maybe you need to set three alarm clocks, or ask your husband or a roommate to wake you, *and* have a friend give you a good-morning call. No action is too drastic!

Another helpful form of accountability is to track the amount of time you spend with the Lord each day and share that data with someone else. The goal here is not to promote legalism, but rather to strive to be faithful in Bible reading and prayer. Seeing on paper the actual time spent can provide an objective and sometimes painful gauge. It doesn't tell us everything about our times with the Lord. However, it can answer two important questions: "To what degree am I actually seeking God?" and "What would growth in time spent with God actually look like?" This exercise is only a suggestion. It's not something we all do all the time, but it is a helpful tool if you are struggling with consistency in sitting and listening to the Lord.

Where to Start

Maybe you've just joined The 5 AM Club and purchased an alarm clock that wakes the neighbors, and you are sitting on the edge of your overstuffed chair, eager to hear from the Lord. Only you don't know where to start. God is gracious to meet us when we open his Word and seek his face through prayer. However, developing a plan for systematically reading portions of Scripture and being faithful in prayer can be of great benefit.

While God is speaking to us through all of Scripture, it's helpful to have a Bible reading plan. In the nineteenth century, Robert Murray M'Cheyne developed a method for reading through the entire Bible once, and the Psalms and New Testament twice, in a year.[5] We have all used modified versions of this plan and find it to be helpful.

And instead of speed reading like you would an eighth-grade literature assignment, take time to listen—meditate—on the words in front of you. One simple method is to write down two sentences, one beginning with "God" and the other starting with "I." To complete your "God" sentence, ask yourself, "What do these verses reveal about God?" For your "I" sentence, you can ask two questions: "What do I learn about myself in relation to God from these verses?" and "What do I resolve to do in response to God's revelation of himself in these verses?" Oh, and you're not limited to one "God" and "I" sentence each—write as many as you like![6]

Then spend time in prayer. Worship God for the aspects of his character that he's revealed in the verses you've just read. Thank him for the many facets of his grace you've glimpsed in the passage. Ask for his assistance to respond in obedience to his Word. And likewise, pray for others.

To further enhance your conviction of the importance of meeting with God and your understanding of what it means to sit at the Savior's feet, we urge you to read Donald Whitney's *Spiritual Disciplines for the Christian Life*[7] and John Piper's *When I Don't Desire God*.[8] These two books will inspire and help you become truly proficient at sitting still.

Also, may we have a word with all you moms of infants and young children? Listen: we know. We understand. We've all been there. You're eager to sit and listen at Jesus's feet. You'd love nothing better. It's just that some days there doesn't seem to be any time for sitting and listening. When it comes to "one of those days," we want to encourage you to follow the example of mom Jean Fleming and "do what you can."

Donald Whitney describes Jean as a woman whose "longings for the things of God reached as high as ever" even when, due to caring for three children in diapers, "her time and energy had new and severe limits."[9] If you are experiencing similar limitations, don't despair over what you can't do, but consider what you *can* do.

For starters, look for some time in the day when you can sit and listen—even if it is only for fifteen minutes. Ask your husband to help you out, or take a few minutes during your baby's nap. In between the sit-and-listen times, get creative.

Put Scripture cards in strategic places (like over the kitchen sink or the changing table). Listen to a worship CD or a sermon online. Pray while you're feeding the baby or walking the living room floor in the middle of the night. Purchase an audio version of the Bible for use in the car or at home. And—really get radical—turn off the television or radio for a while!

You see, it's not so hard. There are many ways to sit and listen throughout the day; you only need to take advantage of them. While this season is extra tricky at times, we must be wary of spiritual apathy. Otherwise, we might find our passion for Christ dim when we finally emerge from diapers and bottles. Let's be diligent to "do what we can," however little that may be.

Guilt Free

We said it at the beginning and hopefully made it clear throughout this chapter: sitting at Jesus's feet is the essential tip to becoming a true shopper of time. It is not, however, a way to gain or lose God's approval.

As believers, we are justified—declared righteous, forgiven, and accepted by God—through grace alone, by faith alone, in Christ alone. We do not earn or forfeit our justification before God based on our performance. Our faithfulness to sit and listen, our diligence to seek the Lord through prayer and Scripture, our efforts to make the best use of the time— none of these is sufficient to earn God's acceptance.

Ephesians 2:8–9 makes it plain: "For by grace you have been saved through faith. And this is not your own doing; it is the gift of God, not a result of works, so that no one may boast." We must keep this in mind as we resolve to sit still at the Savior's feet. We must never assume that our progress or our consistency becomes the means to earn our Lord's forgiveness. We are accepted by God, not by choosing the good portion or by being efficient shoppers of time, but because of Jesus's perfect life, death, and resurrection. B. B. Warfield emphatically hammers home this point:

> There is nothing in us or done by us, at any stage of our earthly development, because of which we are acceptable to God. We must always be accepted for Christ's sake, or we cannot ever be accepted at all. This is not true of us only when we believe. It is just as true after we have believed. It will continue to be true, as long as we live. . . . It is always on his "blood and righteousness" alone that we can rest.[10]

So, if you are discouraged or condemned by your failure to sit and listen, if you are "troubled by many things," revel in this truth: we have a Savior who died for our sins and it is his "blood and righteousness" alone that make us acceptable to God.

Back to Bethany

Now before we conclude this chapter, let's return to Bethany for a moment. We want to clarify something: Martha is not the "bad girl" in this story. Our Lord did rebuke her, but not for her efforts to serve. Rather, he rebuked her for not choosing what was most important—sitting at Jesus's feet. Charles Spurgeon explained: "We ought to be Martha and Mary in one: we should do much service, and have much communion at the same time. For this we need great grace. It is easier to serve than to commune."[11]

Sitting at Jesus's feet doesn't mean we're free to neglect all our earthly responsibilities. Not a chance. God is clear in Scripture—he's got stuff for us to do. But Mr. Spurgeon is right. It's much easier to do than to sit. It will take far less effort to apply the rest of the practical suggestions in this book than to diligently pursue prayer and the study of God's Word. Thus, we do need great grace to choose, along with Mary, "the good portion."

CHAPTER FOUR

The Third Tip: Sit and Plan

(Taking a Personal Retreat)

The high spot of the Mahaney family vacation—for us women anyway—is Outlet Day. The husbands take the kids and we hit the stores. Appropriately, this shopping excursion always begins at the same southern chophouse where we make short work of that delicacy among appetizers: spinach *queso* dip and chips.

Critical to the success of the day is what happens *while* we're chomping on the chips—the creation of a shopping plan. With about a hundred stores sprawled over who-knows-how-many acres, this requires serious consideration. We discuss which stores we each want to visit in order of importance. Then we map out a strategic course to cover the most ground as quickly as possible (including an ice cream stop halfway through the afternoon).

If we failed to make a plan, the day would be a disaster. A shopping nightmare. We would never get to the really good stores because we'd be lost or sidetracked by the cheesy ones. We'd be worn out from covering the same ground two or three times. We'd end up buying things we didn't need and didn't want and miss out on all the super deals. We'd never make it to the ice cream shop. Scary scenario, isn't it?

Every woman worth her weight in coupons knows that smart shopping requires sitting down and planning first. How much more vital, then, is a strategic plan for the changing seasons of our lives? If we simply allow each new season to come along without charting a course, we could easily be sidetracked by urgent yet unimportant activities. We could wear ourselves out repeating the same mistakes and dealing with the same problems over and over. And we could potentially miss the truly significant opportunities each season has to offer.

None of us wants our life to mirror a substandard shopping trip. And they don't have to! We can make the best use of every season by applying Shopping-for-Time Tip 3: "Sit and Plan." The idea is to set aside an extended time once or twice a year for study, prayer, and evaluation. In other words, take a personal retreat.

Mom started taking personal retreats when Nicole and Kristin were little. As the story goes, Mom was feeling weary and burdened by the demands of motherhood. She lacked perspective and joy. So Dad sent her away for twenty-four hours to study God's Word, read encouraging motherhood books, and devise solutions for her challenging season. She returned home happy, rested, and with renewed vision for mothering. Ever since, Dad's insisted she take two retreats per year.

When we girls reached age eleven or twelve, Mom began taking us on our own annual mini retreat. She'd come prepared with Scriptures to encourage us in our walk with the Lord. We'd talk about our devotions and one way we could grow in godliness. Mom would also draw us out about activities we wanted to pursue and ideas for how we could serve in the church. Then we'd come up with a simple little plan.

As preadolescence turned into middle school, high school, college, single years, and then engagement, Mom faithfully helped us develop a new plan for every season. Now that we're married we take retreats on our own, but we still bring Mom in as a consultant!

Over the years, we've received so much benefit from personal retreats that we're eager to commend this practice to you. We think that applying this Shopping-for-Time tip can help all of us sharpen our priorities and discern the best deals. Then we can confidently say no to many good opportunities in favor of better ones. We can avoid repetitive consequences by correcting problem areas. We can develop strategies for overcoming sin and shore up areas where we are weak. We can strengthen our relationships with others. Guided by God's Word, we can acquire clear direction and purpose for the season in front of us. All these benefits and more can transpire from a personal retreat. So why not give it a try?

A Sample Retreat

In order to sit and plan, you have to hit the pause button on life. You have to get away from everyone and everything clamoring for your attention. Maybe it's for several hours or possibly a full day, or even an overnight, depending on how much time you think you need.

And we suggest you find a place where you can be alone, a place where the boss can't get ahold of you and the kids can't find you. Maybe it's as cheap and simple as a park bench or as plush as a hotel room. You can swap retreats with another mom—she watches your kids and then you return the favor. Or you might ask your husband to disentangle you from the mop and toddler long enough to spend a morning at the local coffee shop. These are just a few ideas. But did we mention it's helpful to be *alone*? As you can probably tell, this requires a little advance preparation. But it's oh-so worth it!

So what do you do once you are alone—besides stare at the wall, twiddle your thumbs, or hum catchy tunes? All that time to fill and no clue how to fill it can actually deter some women from taking a personal retreat. To help you get started, we want to offer Mom's Sit-and-Plan strategy that we've all used to great advantage.

Now, of course you don't have to use this method to evaluate your life. There are an endless number of valid techniques. Most likely your approach will be different, more your style. But we hope this plan will provide a starting point that will spark your own creative ideas.

It's really simple. All you need is your Bible and a computer or pen and paper—whichever you're most comfortable with. Begin by listing your priorities. Here's Mom's list:

- Grow in godliness.
- Love my family.
- Serve in the church.
- Fellowship with Christians.
- Evangelize non-Christians.
- Attend to my work.
- Care for my physical health.

Although your list may look slightly different, it's important that your priorities come from God's Word and not cultural or personal preferences. We should all have similar priorities stemming from our identity as Christian women, even though we may use other words or categories to describe them.

Once you've listed your priorities, create a separate page for each one to use as a worksheet. Then evaluate yourself, prayerfully going through the priorities one at a time. Under each category, assess how you are doing—what is going well and what needs to change. Then consider how you can grow in that key area of your life. After you've completed your evaluation, you'll use this data to come up with a simple plan for your current season.

Do you have your blank worksheets ready and your pen (or fingers) poised? Good. Let's zoom in for a closer look at our priorities.

Priority 1: Grow in Godliness

First Timothy 4:8 asserts: "While bodily training is of some value, godliness is of value in every way, as it holds promise for the present life and also for the life to come." Because godliness is of eminent importance, this is our first priority.

Under this category we should first consider our practice of meeting with God (as covered in the previous chapter) and ask ourselves, "How can I make my devotions more fruitful?" Maybe we are struggling with consistency and need a friend to give us a wake-up call. Or possibly we need to implement a new Bible-reading plan.

Secondly, we must evaluate our progress in personal holiness: "What is one area where I believe God is calling me to grow in godliness?" This may be a pattern of bitterness or judgmentalism about which we have recently been convicted. Maybe our husband or a friend has pointed out an evidence of pride or selfishness. Or we may have been tempted by fear and unbelief in the midst of a trial. Once we discover an area in need of growth, we might look up Scripture verses on this topic. Or we might decide to read a book or an article or ask our husband or a friend for help. Simply taking one step of humility will invite God's grace to help us change.

Priority 2: Love My Family

According to Titus 2:4, a woman's main concern should be to love her family. Therefore, on this page it is helpful to make a list of the names of our immediate family members. If we are married with children, we will want to write down their names. If we still live at home with our parents, we might list them along with our siblings. Possibly we are caretaker for an elderly relative, or we are single with nieces and nephews, or we have grandchildren. Whatever our family configuration, we should list our closest relatives.

After making our list, we should ponder the question, "What is one family relationship I want to give more attention to in this season?" We should begin by considering whether or not we need to address any deficiencies or challenges in our marriage. Or, if we feel one of our children needs special attention, we may start there. It could be that we've realized we need to spend more time with our parents or work on repairing our relationship with one of our siblings.

Once we identify a priority family relationship, we should ask ourselves, "How can I more intentionally show love to this person?" We don't have to develop a complex strategy. Maybe we can block out a regular time to visit our parents, or plan an occasional outing with our nieces, or call up our brother whom we haven't talked to in several months. We might decide to plan a special surprise for our husband or pray more consistently for an unsaved child. Whatever the relationship, whatever the plan—keeping it simple is the key!

Priority 3: Serve in the Church

The church is the center of God's activity on earth today. Therefore, we are to serve faithfully in our local church, or, as 1 Peter 4:10 puts it, "As each has received a gift, use it to serve one another, as good stewards of God's varied grace."

We must consider: "Am I using my gifts to serve in my local church?" Maybe we've neglected such service due to laziness or fear. Perhaps we've been employing our gifts everywhere—the PTA, overtime at the office, an area-women's Bible study—*except* in our local congregation. None of these pursuits should ever crowd out our service in the church. However, making the church a priority doesn't mean we have to sign up for every serving opportunity the pastor mentions from the pulpit. Let's offer our assistance in one or two arenas and be prepared to use our gifts humbly.

Sometimes this question may lead us to evaluate whether we are serving in the most effective ways. Maybe we need to back out of one serving commitment in order to give attention to another. There may also be seasons where the demands of home life may require us to serve less in the church in order to focus more on our family. However, even if our time is limited, we must always be good stewards of our gifts to faithfully serve our local church.

Priority 4: Fellowship with Christians

It's no accident that relationships—with family, other Christians, and unbelievers—comprise three of our seven priorities. People are important! That's why we'll spend the whole next chapter carefully considering our relationships. In the meantime, 1 John 1:7 declares the value of fellowship with other believers in the context of the local church: "If we walk in the light, as he is in the light, we have fellowship with one another, and the blood of Jesus his Son cleanses us from all sin."

"Is there a relationship I need to prioritize for the purpose of fellowship?" If we don't have at least one friend with whom we are "walking in the light," then we should pursue one. Maybe we can ask a godly woman in our church or small group to begin meeting with us once a month. Or maybe we simply need to share our life more openly and humbly with our husband or a dear friend. Of course, if you are a teenager and have a godly mother, there is no better source for fellowship.

Conversely, it is helpful to consider, "Are there relationships that are hindering my fellowship, and how do they need to change?" Maybe we realize that we spend too much time hanging out with unbelievers. We might need to cut back on activities with them in order to make room for relationships with mature Christians. Or possibly we spend a lot of time with Christian friends but our conversation is superficial. Walking in the light can be as simple as asking a spiritual question or confessing a sin when we get together.

Priority 5: Evangelize Non-Christians

The pastors at Nicole's church recently used a helpful phrase to encourage their members in evangelism: "Let each one who has received grace reach one who needs grace." *Each one reach one.* Evangelism is to be a priority for all Christians. When he issued the Great Commission, Jesus said, "Go into all the world and proclaim the gospel to the whole creation" (Mark 16:15).

Practicing this priority will look different for each of

us, depending on our season. A college student is probably surrounded by unsaved classmates, just as a woman employed in the secular workforce may have many non-Christian colleagues. A homemaker lives next door to unbelieving neighbors and comes in regular contact with unsaved members of her community. Instead of feeling overwhelmed by the number of non-Christians around us, we should prayerfully think, "Who is one person I can develop a friendship with for the purpose of sharing the gospel?"

Priority 6: Attend to My Work

We are all familiar with the command to "work heartily, as for the Lord and not for men" (Col. 3:23). Whatever our work is—homemaking, studying, pursuing a career—we should ask, "Am I doing the right work?" Often this is an easy one to answer. If we are wives and mothers, then homemaking is our primary work. If we are students, then school is a non-negotiable priority. If we are single women, or single moms, then earning a living is a necessity.

Occasionally, however, we come to a new season when answering this question is more complex. We might realize we need to take a lighter college course load to focus on church priorities or family needs. Or possibly we need to assume an extra part-time job to pay for tuition costs. Perhaps we are considering a career change. If we have a family and are also employed, we need to evaluate whether or not our secondary work is hindering our primary work.

Once we are confident we are doing the right work, then we need to ask, "What is one way I can be more effective or efficient in the work God has called me to do?" Of course a million ideas probably come to mind, but we would be wise to limit ourselves to one or two!

Priority 7: Care for My Physical Body

Last but not least is the priority of caring for our physical body. First Corinthians 6:19 explains why this is important: "Do you not know that your body is a temple of the Holy Spirit within you, whom you have from God? You are not your own." Because we are not our own, we must be mindful of our health. A balanced diet, good exercise, proper rest, and regular doctors' visits are all ways we can take proper care of our physical body. But 1 Timothy 4:8 protects us from an obsession over our physical fitness and appearance. It reminds us that "bodily training is of *some* value" but not of "value in every way"—as is godliness.

So holding these two verses (1 Cor. 6:19 and 1 Tim. 4:8), one in each hand, we should ask ourselves: "Am I giving too much or too little attention to the care of my physical body?" If we have been overindulging in unhealthy food or skipping necessary sleep or avoiding the doctor, then maybe we need to give this area *more* attention. However, if exercise is crowding out our time with the Lord, or if we are more passionate about health food than the gospel or more concerned with staying thin than serving others, then our physical body should cease to be our primary focus.

Once we have determined whether we need to give more or less attention to our physical body, let's decide, "What action must I take in order to appropriately care for my body?" We might need to join a gym or cancel our gym membership, start a diet or go to the doctor, or simply spend less time in front of the mirror and more face time in God's Word.

One Thing

Is your head spinning yet? If you find all these priorities and questions even a wee bit overwhelming, we are standing by to relieve the pressure. Here's how: don't try to change in every area all at once.

This is extremely important. If you target too many areas for growth, you may fail to make progress in any of them and end up more discouraged than when you began. However, if you develop a plan to change in one area, you will be surprised at the dramatic difference it will make. If the only action you pursue is to wake up early and seek God, no corner of your life will go untouched. If you simply reach out to one non-Christian neighbor, you will experience joy that lasts for eternity. Remember this: even if you only change in one area, you will be doing more than if you hadn't sat down to plan at all.

So ask yourself this final question: "What one or two priorities do I want to focus on for the next three to six months, and what steps will I take to grow in each area?"

If you're wondering why we suggest considering seven priorities for change and then recommend focusing on only one or two, the reason is this: taking the time to comprehensively evaluate our life causes the truly vital issues to rise to the top. In other words, we discover which area is most in need of attention and which steps for change will advance us the furthest. Each season offers only a few best deals, so in order to be successful shoppers of time, we must identify those best deals and buy them up.

A Sample Plan

After settling on one or two priority areas to which we will give our attention, we next consider a plan for change.

Often this is the most time-intensive yet fruitful portion of a personal retreat. Here's how Nicole mapped out a strategy for change on one of her recent retreats. She had determined that mothering Jack was the priority in need of special focus at that time.

First, she prayerfully assessed her heart and conduct as a mother. Through recent conversations with her husband, Mom, and friends, she was convicted about a lack of consistency in discipline. So she reviewed several of her favorite parenting books and selected verses and quotes on this topic. These she typed out in a computer document for review during her morning devotions.

Then she turned her attention to Jack's training. She and Steve were both concerned by Jack's tendency to argue instead of to obey immediately. Nicole brainstormed about how to make her guidelines and commands more clear, her language more simple and biblical, and how to prevent situations in which Jack was tempted to disobey.

Jack was also due for some lessons in dinnertime etiquette, she figured, specifically, learning to sit still until everyone was finished eating and to participate in conversation by asking good questions. So she came up with a few ideas for Steve to consider and implement in teaching Jack.

Finally, Nicole reviewed Jack's daily and weekly schedule—what was working well and what wasn't. Out of this evaluation came a new morning routine and several changes to the weekly calendar. She also focused on specific aspects of Jack's schedule by studying a preschool curriculum, checking into a soccer program, and figuring out the best spots for "daddy-time."

By dedicating time to sit and develop a plan for Jack, Nicole was able to take several big steps forward in her effectiveness as a mother. Of course, if she had attempted to develop a similar plan for every priority, she would have been overwhelmed. But Nicole determined that the best deal of that season was to be found in the mothering department.

Once we've developed a plan, we'll need to take a number of next steps in order to implement it. For example, Nicole came away with to-do's such as "purchase school supplies," "reschedule time of weekly play-date," "ask Steve about soccer program," and many more. It is a good idea to transfer these action items to whatever tools we use to organize our daily life *before* we conclude our retreat. This will help us turn our good plans into reality.

Our Savior's Example

Maybe we've piqued your interest with this personal retreat idea. The thought of correcting problem areas, gaining clarity, and finding the best deals in each season appeals to you. But, on the other hand, your calendar and to-do list are screaming to be heard. And you think: "A personal retreat is all well and good, but I'm too busy. There are too many demands on my time, too many people counting on me. Perhaps I'll consider it when life slows down."

But just as it would be foolish for us to tackle Outlet Day without mapping out a plan, so we can't afford to put off charting a course for life's seasons because we are too busy. The pressures of life are, in fact, the very reason we need to sit and plan.

And when we do so, we are simply following our Savior's example when he walked this earth. As we read the Gospels, we notice that Jesus frequently withdrew from his responsibilities in order to wait prayerfully for his Father's instructions. "But now even more the report about him went abroad, and great crowds gathered to hear him and to be healed of their infirmities. But he would withdraw to desolate places and pray" (Luke 5:15–16).

Prior to these verses in Luke, Jesus had just healed a man of leprosy. Thus, many more people with physical and spiritual needs were flocking to him. Even so, he withdrew to pray. Now, if Jesus—God Incarnate—needed to go away to a lonely place to prayerfully discern his Father's will, *do we think we can pull it off any other way?*

Author Jean Fleming, whom we met in the last chapter, also makes a case from the life of Jesus for the importance of personal retreats:

> Some people tell me they feel uncomfortable with the idea of a personal retreat. After all, the needs around us are so great, the opportunities for service so compelling. How do we reconcile taking time away from the heat of battle when so much needs to be done? It is precisely because the needs are so great and life so short that I take personal retreats. Retreat is the way to advance. I know this is true because of the way Jesus lived.
>
> Life for Jesus was short and busy, too. He lived on earth fully aware that the clock was ticking away. Jesus had only three-and-a-half years for public ministry, but this didn't keep Him from taking personal retreats. Jesus modeled and taught regular withdrawal into God's presence. The Gospel of Mark, the most action-packed account of the life of Jesus, shows Him continually pulling back from opportunities to minister so that He could pray and listen to His Father. His life illustrates the perfect life; one of retreat followed by intense involvement in the world.[12]

When we're tempted to think life's demands preclude us from taking a personal retreat, let's remember our Savior's perfect example. It's precisely because the needs are so great and life so short, because the seasons keep rolling in without a pause, that we need to take time to sit and plan. So before you rush back to the day's demands, may we suggest you get out your calendar and schedule a personal retreat?

CHAPTER FIVE

The Fourth Tip: Consider People

(Evaluating Relationships Carefully)

There's actually a sequel to the Mahaney vacation Outlet Day: Outlet Day II. Same cast of characters—the four of us girls—except we add the men (our four husbands and Chad) this time. We still consume the same spinach *queso* dip (only a whole lot more of it!) at the same chophouse. But when we emerge into the bright sunlight to gaze upon the rows of stores, the day takes on a slightly different feel.

While there's an intentional plan for each of these shopping excursions, the point of the original Outlet Day, Outlet Day I, is to shop for a wide range of needs whereas Outlet Day II has a more specific focus.

On Outlet Day I, we girls thoroughly comb all our favorite stores, look at price tags, rifle through sales racks, and swap opinions. "Is two for twenty a good deal?" "Will this shirt go with that pair of pants I have?" "Look at that hideous couch!" We try on ten pairs of shoes and put one on hold while we check out two more shoe stores. We spend at least an hour at the cosmetic counter testing different shades of lipstick. We try to find winter clothes for our children—never mind that it's ninety degrees outside. We indulge ourselves with a visit to the Coach store, even though the budget prohibits us from purchasing a bag.

C.J. (Dad), however, sets the agenda and pace for Outlet Day II. Like most men, shopping doesn't rank among his top ten favorite activities. But he takes unique delight in blessing his family. So, in order to spend a minimum amount of time at the outlets while bringing maximum joy to his children, he's come up with a strategy that makes everyone happy.

"Your mother and I want to give each of you fifty dollars to buy one gift of choice," he announces. (Big grins all around the family circle.) "The only stipulation is this: you have sixty minutes to spend it. You must be back here by 3:15 with your purchase in hand or you'll forfeit the money." (At this point, watch Kristin, the serious shopper of the family. Her muscles tense like a runner at the starting block and her eyes squint with resolute focus.) "Ready, set, go!"

Now if, by chance, you happen to be at an outlet mall and notice people running in and out of stores as if their life depended on it, don't be alarmed. It's probably just someone from our family with fifty bucks on the line.

Sit and Plan II

Two different days. Two different objectives. Both are strategic. Both are intentional. Outlet Day I encompasses all variety of shopping needs. Outlet Day II is about one specific purchase.

In the previous chapter, we introduced Mom's Sit-and-Plan exercise. It encompasses all of our major priorities. In this chapter, we want to offer another exercise as an addendum of sorts. Think of it as "Sit and Plan II." Here we'll consider a single, yet very significant, aspect of our lives: relationships. You can use this evaluation alongside your personal retreat plan or on its own. But for the next few pages, we want to take a closer look at our people priorities.

A Relationship List

As women, we are, by nature, relational creatures. We thrive on interaction with others and wither apart from it. Our world is primarily centered on our family and friends.

Yet, we are often more passive and receptive than we are intentional and purposeful in our relationships. We may allow people to drift in and out of our lives. We don't usually pause to consider why we pursue a certain friendship or neglect another. Emotions and feelings often dictate the way we go about relationships.

However, people are so important and consume such a big chunk of our time that in order to be prudent time shoppers, we should give them special attention. We must prayerfully evaluate our relational priorities in the light of God's priorities. That's why Tip 4 is "Consider People." Do our relationships—the time we spend with our family and the friends we pursue—bring glory to God?

Of course, following our relationship with God, family should hold top billing. Our husband, our children, our parents, and our siblings should be the recipients of our most ardent affection and sacrificial service. These relationships are of such significance that we wrote our first two books about them. *Feminine Appeal*[13] portrays the role of the wife and mother, and *Girl Talk*[14] delves into the mother-daughter relationship.

Then there's the whole romantic guy-girl thing—talk about time-consuming, thought preoccupying, emotionally charged relationships! It would take an entire book even to begin to tackle this topic. Fortunately, our good friend Joshua Harris has already written three. So consult *I Kissed Dating Goodbye*,[15] *Boy Meets Girl*,[16] and *Sex Is Not the Problem (Lust Is)*,[17] for a road map to walking wisely as you relate to men.

While family and romantic relationships will come into view, we want to focus primarily on friendships in this chapter. To "consider people"—you guessed it—we need to make a list. Just as in the previous chapter we put down our priorities, this time we're going to list our relationships. Simply write out the names of all the people in your relational network, beginning with your family. If you've never made a list like this before, you may be in for some surprising discoveries about yourself and how you relate to others. We think you'll come to see how careful consideration can greatly enrich your relationships.

Friends to Choose

Have you made your list? Great! Now you may be wondering, "How do I go about evaluating these relationships? What criteria do I use?" Thankfully we haven't been left to guess or, worse yet, consult our fickle feelings on the matter. God's Word provides clarity. It exhorts us to be intentional. Proverbs 12:26 tells us that: "The righteous should choose his friends carefully" (NKJV). So what kinds of friends should we choose?

Let's briefly fly over Scripture to discover which friends (in addition to family, of course) should be on our list.

1) Friends Who Sharpen

Our idea of a first-rate friend might be someone who's easy to get along with, laughs at the same movie lines, shares our opinions on fashion and food, can finish our sentences, sticks by us in the rough going, and is free to hang out on a Friday night. All plus-points to be sure. But Scripture says there's a friend quality of much greater value. Actually, it's one we can't afford to do without. The best kind of friend, according to Proverbs 27:17, is one who sharpens us as "iron sharpens iron" (NKJV).

In Hebrews 10:24 we find a less metaphorical description of this ideal friend as someone who "[stirs us] up . . . to love and good works." We need to have at least one—and preferably many—friends who inspire us to serve, provoke us to love, help us grow in godliness, correct us, strengthen our faith, and spur us on to passion for the Savior. So do any "sharpening" friends appear on our list? If not, we need to find some—and fast!

It may be we simply need to take a current relationship in a new direction. One or more friends on our list may prove to be a sharpening influence after all. We only have to ask! If we invite a Christian friend to point out our sin, encourage us in the gospel, and stir us up to love and good deeds, chances are they won't turn us down.

But maybe, as we assess the spiritual maturity of the people on our list, we realize we need to add some godly friends. This may require a step or two outside the old comfort zone. But even if it's a little awkward at first, we need to initiate friendships with people we're confident will sharpen us. For our friendship list will be woefully incomplete without this most valuable kind of friend.

2) Friends Who Mentor

Do you know that there should be an educational aspect to our friendships with other women? If scary images of algebra classes come to mind, relax. We're not talking about formal education but about training in biblical womanhood. Titus 2:3–5 says that the "older women [in the church] . . . are to teach what is good, and so train the young women to love their husbands and children, to be self-controlled, pure, working at home, kind, and submissive to their own husbands."

In this school of godly womanhood there is a charge to both students and teachers. Those of us who are younger should be studying and learning. We are the women in training. We ought to aggressively seek out other women to help us grow in the admirable qualities of biblical femininity. And if we possess the teaching credentials of an older woman—proven character and a fruitful life—we should be faithful to pass on our experience and wisdom to those behind us.

So let's take a peek at our list. Young women, we should ask ourselves: "Do I have a friend from whom I am learning some aspect of biblical womanhood?" And older women, we should consider: "Am I faithfully imparting biblical womanhood to at least one friend?"

Teenage girls, if you have a godly mom, she's to be your mentor. For the rest of us younger women, let's ask a mature woman in our church to teach us what she knows about caring for the home, or glorifying God in the workplace, or walking in purity. A friend who mentors or a friend we mentor deserves a prominent spot on our relationship list.

3) Friends Who Need Friends

It's so easy, isn't it, to get comfortable with our close friends, the gang, the group—dare we say it, *the clique*? While long-time friends are a significant blessing from the Lord, we are also called to reach out to the new person, the lonely, the foreigner. "Let brotherly love continue. Do not neglect to show hospitality to strangers," exhorts Hebrews 13:1–2.

Remember what it was like when you were new? What it felt like not to know anyone? To see other women chatting excitedly and to have no one to talk to? Ever been left out or forgotten? To choose our friends carefully means we must guard against selfishness and laziness. We should consider how to show sisterly love to someone who needs a friend.

So let's take a look around us: "Who is one new friend I should add to my list, and how can I reach out to her?" Reaching out can be as simple as introducing ourselves to a visitor at church, or inviting a quiet woman out for coffee, or including someone new at our weekly lunch with friends. Let's help new friends not feel new for very long.

4) Friends Who Need Salvation

In Colossians 4:5–6 Paul describes how we are to relate to the fourth kind of friend who should make our list: "Walk in wisdom toward outsiders, making the best use of the time. Let your speech always be gracious, seasoned with salt, so that you may know how you ought to answer each person." Did you notice the similar language here to that of our book's theme verse, Ephesians 5:15–16? Both refer to walking wisely and "making the best use of the time."

One of the ways we can make the best use of the time is by wise conduct toward unbelievers. Obviously, in writing this verse Paul assumes that we have contact with those outside the faith. So if everyone on your list has grown up in a Christian home or been a Christian for twenty years, you're missing someone.

Often it can be so easy for us as women to get consumed by our school, our work, or our responsibilities at home, that we neglect the priority of evangelism. It's like we walk around campus, through the office cubicles, in and out of the grocery store, and across the street with our head down and blinders on. But we are supposed to be reaching out and having gracious, gospel-motivated conversations with non-Christians. You don't know any? They are not that hard to find! All you have to do is look up.

Friends who sharpen and mentor. Friends who need a friend. Friends who need salvation. Not only should they all make our relationship list—they should be a priority!

But don't misunderstand. We're not trying to say that friendship is all duty and no fun. God not only approves of laughter, pleasure, and companionship—they actually flow from his gracious character (Acts 14:17; 1 Tim. 6:17; James 1:17). So we can trust that although work is involved, when we choose friends according to God's criteria, these blessings and more will result.

Friends to Leave

Scripture not only enlightens us about whom we should include in our circle of friends; it also warns us who should not be a part of our relational network. Proverbs 13:20 again echoes our Ephesians 5:15–16 language by informing us, "Whoever walks with the wise will become wise." But it goes on to warn, "The companion of fools will suffer harm."

We must soberly assess our list. Are the foolish, the

ungodly, or the rebellious among our friends? Do we gravitate toward and enjoy hanging out with people who love the world more than they love the Savior? If so, we are in dangerous company. For just as surely as godly friends bring blessing, fools bring harm.

What kind of harm? Scripture tells us in 1 Corinthians 15:33: "Do not be deceived: 'Bad company ruins good morals.'" Someone wisely stated: "The simple lesson is that we become like those whose company we keep." When we make friends with the fool, we gradually, yet inevitably, become like them.

And what's truly dangerous is our tendency to think this won't happen to us, to think that Scripture, in fact, doesn't know what it's talking about. We believe we can walk closely with the ungodly and yet remain untainted. We can handle it. But that's why we are warned in 1 Corinthians, "Do not be deceived." For the reality is that we don't hang out with the foolish and become more wise. We don't consort with the rebellious and become more obedient. We don't associate with the worldly and become more godly.

So if we've discovered bad company on our list, we must cease to walk with them. We must kindly—but hastily—extricate ourselves from any relationship that is an ungodly influence in our life. Not only that, but we must seek to fall in step with some wise friends as soon as possible.

"How do I tell someone I can't be her friend anymore?" you ask. "What if I hurt her feelings?" Better her feelings than your life. Of course, this can be delicate. We would encourage you to get help from a godly mother, husband, or wise friend. But remember, severing an ungodly friendship will not only keep you from harm; it may be the event God uses to draw that person to himself.

Priority Relationships

It's important to choose friends carefully because friendships take time, and we want to make sure our time is wisely spent. We want to be faithful shoppers of time. So now that we've determined from God's Word who should make our friendship list, we want to take a second look and evaluate, "Does our time—our involvement and investment—with each person reflect the priority this relationship should hold in this season of life?"

While we may have the *right* people on our list, it's possible to devote the *wrong* amount of time to certain relationships. For example, we may have many godly friends, all of whom spur us on to love and good deeds. Only problem is, we have *too* many friends—so many that we can't keep up with them all, so many that they crowd out other priorities and significant relationships.

Or maybe our social circle is small, and we spend every waking hour with one or two friends. We text message and e-mail and go to the store together and hang out every evening. We're joined at the hip, as they say, and there's no room for other important relationships to squeeze in.

It's also possible for someone to top our relationship list and yet receive a disproportionately small amount of our time. Of course all of us agree that our family is most important to us. We must consider, however, whether our devotion of time to their care reflects the priority we believe they should hold.

Finally, we must recognize that changing seasons will also mean changing relationships. Carefully considering our people priorities isn't a one-time exercise. We don't create our relationship list and then place it in a safety deposit box, for as one season makes room for another, friendships may also need to adjust. Marriage, children, extended family responsibilities, ministry opportunities—all may necessitate that we spend less time on certain relationships and devote more to others. But as it states in Ecclesiastes, there is a time for every season and matter under heaven (3:1).

Now that we've carefully considered who should be on our relationship list and how much time they should receive, let's ask ourselves: "What specific practical changes do we need to make so that we are investing in the right people for the right amount of time?" Don't rush this, but take as long as you need to prayerfully discern the answer to this question.

Whom We Walk With

We all make lists—grocery lists, packing lists, to-do lists— but chances are you've never made a relationship list before. It's our prediction, however, that your relationship list may become one of the most helpful lists you ever compile. Not only is it a wonderful opportunity to give thanks to God for the blessing of family and friends, but it can also help provide clarity, insight, and direction regarding friendships that you might have missed out on if you had never made this list. For in order to be wise shoppers of time, we must not only look carefully at *how* we walk but with *whom* we walk.

CHAPTER SIX

The Fifth Tip: Plan to Depend

(Being Productive in Daily Life)

On a recent Wednesday morning, a small group of moms, babies, and toddlers gathered at Janelle's townhouse for a playgroup. They brought diaper bags and sack lunches and there were hugs and laughter (and baby cries) all around. Janelle made cookies.

"But no need to bring drinks," Janelle had told them. That's because Janelle's eclectic, boldly colored living room is dominated by a rather untraditional piece of dècor—a full-size, vintage (c. 1969) soda machine. If your eyebrows just hit your hairline, that's only because you don't know Janelle. It took five grown men to maneuver this behemoth into the pint-size room. But it's truly a grand sight to behold. And, it still works! A couple hours before guests arrive in their home, Janelle plugs it in to chill the cans (it lights up!). Then, if you insert ten cents (sometimes twenty—it has a mind of its own) it will dispense your beverage of choice: Coke, Diet Coke, Fresca, Sprite, or A&W Root Beer.

We women are a little like Janelle's vending machine, except that we provide solutions instead of cold cans of Coke. Need a meal? Need a ride? Need a babysitter? Need a substitute? Need a shoulder to cry on? We're your women! Just put in your request, and we'll dispense the solution to your need.

Of course everyone needs something from us, and they usually need it right away. But, hopefully, by now we all agree that we must not base our decisions solely on the needs of others. We can do a lot of things—meet a lot of needs—and yet miss out on the best deals of the season. That's why it's profitable to rise early and sit at Jesus's feet—buying up that "best deal" first thing in the morning—and why it's clarifying to get away and sit and plan on a personal retreat.

But it's so easy to come down from the mountaintop of a personal retreat, or emerge from our morning devotions, and fall right back into dispensing solutions. Our priorities, the best deals, get overrun by the horde of needs demanding our attention. And the peace, joy, and anticipation we basked in just a short time before quickly evaporates.

The question is, how do we buy up the best deals and maintain peace and joy amidst the needs, the interruptions, the unexpected events of daily life? We must have a strategy, which brings us to our fifth and final tip: "Plan to Depend." By consulting this tip, we can make our good intentions a reality, avoid a solution-dispensing lifestyle, and avail ourselves of God's grace each and every day.

Daily Plans

For starters, we highly recommend you develop (if you haven't already) a daily planning system that works for you. We all need a method to make our plans a reality. And we all need a place to store our appointments, tasks, goals, and lists of information in an accessible and usable format.

Our keep-it-all-together tools are often a calendar and a to-do list of some kind—tangible items that we use to plan our days. Your method for planning might be simple enough to require only a legal pad and pen along with the free calendar from your local realtor. Or you may have a sophisticated system that utilizes a laptop computer, a BlackBerry, or some other electronic device. But it's whatever works for you.

Nicole's daily planning system—her entire life, in fact—is on her laptop computer (which is a little scary considering how often she spills drinks and how infrequently she backs up). Mom also uses a laptop, but she prefers to print out her daily schedule and keep her calendar in a spiral notebook. She's still a tad wary of technology. Kristin can't use a computer for her daily planning system because her youngest son, Owen, has a thing for plucking off keys. She uses a funky "mom's planner" complete with babysitter page and kid's seasonal schedule. Janelle also owns a laptop, but a computer is way too uncreative for her daily planning system. She uses a giant sketchbook together with her big bucket of markers (every color in the rainbow).

Between us we represent four very different planning systems. And there are many more tools and methods available today. Numerous intelligent and effective books have been written on the topic of organization, and many individuals have perfected their suggestions in real life. That's why we're not going to elaborate further here.

But if you don't have a functioning daily planning system, browse your local bookshop or pester an organized friend to explain her method to you. Be prepared to experiment; you may not hit on the ideal plan the first time. It's well worth the effort, however, because an effective planning system enables us to maintain consistency and order in daily life. Once our system is in place, the following three suggestions will help us squeeze the most benefit out of each and every day.

1) Take Fifteen Minutes

For a book about shopping for time, we talk a lot about sitting—sitting at Jesus's feet, sitting to plan the season's priorities and to evaluate relationships. Well, we're going to do it one more time. Because sitting for a few minutes each morning can considerably affect the trajectory of our day. We base this claim on a businessman's helpful little rule, the 15:4 rule:

> Spending fifteen minutes thinking about what you are going to do before you start will save four hours of wasted time later on. Any individual who has thought through her workday, set priorities, and organized the day's tasks is likely to accomplish far more than someone who randomly moves through the day.[18]

According to the 15:4 rule, when we deposit a few minutes into morning planning, we'll yield significant returns in time and productivity all day long. Besides, when we think about what we're going to do *before* we start, we can be confident we're buying up the best deals and dispensing the most helpful solutions.

Ignore this little rule, however, and we potentially throw away time that was free for the taking. Not pausing for a few minutes to plot our day's course is like running to the grocery store without glancing in the fridge or pantry or making a list. We arrive back home only to discover we forgot two items. Forty-five minutes and one return-trip later, we've completed our shopping. But imagine what we could have done with that extra time!

On the other hand, if we're faithful to plan first thing each morning, we'll conserve loads of valuable time. We may realize that our hair salon is in the same shopping center as the post office, or figure out that we can fit in an important phone call while walking the dog. Maybe we plan to study terms for a test while at the gym or finish a reading assignment in the doctor's waiting room. If we make the 15:4 rule a daily ritual, just imagine how much time we'll save in a month, a year, a lifetime!

2) Choose the Best Time

Practicing the 15:4 rule opens the door to another productivity option. It gives us a chance to decide the best time to complete each task.

First, consider what optimal time corresponds to each type of task. For many of us, it is ideal to schedule tasks that require more intense thinking or energy (e.g., composing a delicate e-mail, preparing for a business presentation, scrubbing the bathroom floor, grocery shopping) earlier in the day, when our mind and body are at peak energy. Then we can relegate the brainless or less strenuous tasks (e.g., folding laundry, looking for new recipes, filling out forms, calling a relative) to the end of the day. This way, we are utilizing our physical and mental resources most efficiently.

Secondly, and perhaps even more importantly, it helps us fight that pesky enemy of peace and productivity: procrastination. Here's how it works. When you sit down in the morning and look at your to-do list, ask yourself, "Which task am I most likely to avoid?" Then resolve to take care of it *first*. We know. It's hard to do. But these thoughts from Alexander

MacLaren may help you view unpleasant responsibilities a little differently:

> No unwelcome tasks become any the less unwelcome by putting them off till tomorrow. It is only when they are behind us and done, that we begin to find that there is a sweetness to be tasted afterwards, and that the remembrance of unwelcome duties unhesitatingly done is welcome and pleasant. Accomplished, they are full of blessing, and there is a smile on their faces as they leave us. Undone, they stand threatening and disturbing our tranquility, and hindering our communion with God. If there be lying before you any bit of work from which you shrink, go straight up to it, and do it at once. The only way to get rid of it is to do it.[19]

Only imagine how happy our day will be, once we've rid ourselves of that disagreeable task!

3) Eat an Elephant

This final suggestion will assist us in tackling those outsized projects—the ones that simply don't fit into the sixteen waking hours of a given day. Instead of being intimidated by their sheer size and running the other direction, we can break them down into small, manageable segments. Plan to do a little bit each day. Or, as the phrase goes, "Eat an elephant one bite at a time." In the book *Life Management for Busy Women*, Elizabeth George explains her approach:

> I'm working my way through my house by my own method. I call it the "one foot" method. I clean out at least one drawer, one shelf, or one foot of space every day. And it's usually done during transitional time, while I'm doing something else, like warming something in the microwave,

waiting for the coffee to brew, heating food on the stove, talking on the phone, etc.[20]

Organizing an entire house is a daunting task—an elephant—but one that can be accomplished by eating it a bite at a time. So what's the elephant in your life: boxes full of old photographs, piles of unsorted papers, a big thick book? Simply subdivide this elephant into smaller portions and eat them one bite, one day at a time.

When Plans Go Awry

While a daily planning system and smart planning habits will enable us to make the best use of the time in the ordinary course of daily living, we know life doesn't always conform to our plans. Minor inconveniences disrupt and major trials can completely derail the best of goals and intentions. Or, as our shopping-for-time theme verse reminds us, "the days are evil." So what do we do when life messes with our plans?

Interruptions

You know how it goes. For weeks you've been preparing for a big presentation at work only to wake up with the flu. Or you need to study for a test but your mom asks you to babysit your little sister. Perhaps you finish a cleaning project only to have your two-year-old color all over the wall—with permanent marker. Maybe you have tasks stacked up from morning till night, and a neighbor unexpectedly drops by for a long chat. At these moments, this perspective-altering thought from C. S. Lewis can be of assistance:

> The great thing, if one can, is to stop regarding all the unpleasant things as interruptions of one's "own" or

"real" life. The truth is of course that what one calls the
interruptions are precisely one's real life—the life God is
sending one day by day: what one calls one's "real life" is
a phantom of one's own imagination. This at least is what
I see at moments of insight: but it's hard to remember it
all the time.[21]

What a difference it can make when we call to mind this
biblical truth! All the interruptions—they aren't interruptions
after all. They are sovereign deliveries. The unpleasant things
are God's perfect plan for our day. Contemplating this bit of
wisdom can bring a smile to our face, even when our schedule has gone off track and our to-do list remains unfinished.
Because, as Psalm 118:24 so cheerily puts it: "This is the day
that the LORD has made; let us rejoice and be glad in it."

This is the day that the Lord has made. And he's orches-
trated every unpleasant interruption—um, sovereign delivery—for our good. Let's pray that God will help us to remember
this truth. Because Mr. Lewis was right: it's easy to forget.

Busy Seasons

Sure, interruptions are bothersome. They can even be distress-
ing at times. But what if our problem isn't an isolated interruption in a single day, but weeks or months where one or more
big happening threatens to crowd out almost everything else?
Think Christmas . . . finals . . . travel . . . business presentation . . . start of the school year . . . new baby. How do we
decide what should and shouldn't get done and deal with the
guilt and anxiety besides? Three simple principles can help us
navigate uniquely busy seasons.

1) *Separate* the really-do-matter items from the really-
don't-matter items. *Then take care of the really-do-matter*

items first. For example, when we hit hectic seasons as home-makers, Mom has taught us girls that after sitting at Jesus's feet, we should attend to three priorities before anything else. (1) Our husband: "What one thing would please my husband the most?" (2) Our children: "What one issue in my child's life needs consistent attention?" (3) Our food and laundry: "Regardless of how dirty my house is, or how many piles of clutter have accumulated, or whether or not the beds are made—as long as my family has nourishing food to eat and clean clothes to wear, their basic needs will be taken care of."

2) *Simplify* the really-do-matter items where possible. Examine your essential to-do list and ask, "How can I make these tasks easier?" Take your husband's dress shirts to the dry cleaners. Use paper products at mealtime. Order pizza for dinner.

3) *Size up* our limitations. As C.J. (Dad) likes to remind us, "Only God gets his to-do list done each day. We are not God. We are finite creatures with serious limitations." Only God accomplishes everything he needs to do, in exactly the way he intends, in precisely the right amount of time. Only God! This truth helps us see the arrogant absurdity of expecting to complete our own to-do list. It frees us to humble ourselves and draw upon God's strength to simply do what we can in busy seasons.

Inevitable Trials

Because the days are evil, trials are inevitable. And when they strike, the last thing on our minds is our to-do list. But needs don't always give us time to grieve. The children still have to be fed, or the boss expects us at work, or the professor won't delay the test. How do we deal with what needs to be done when all we want to do is sit down and cry? This simple poem offers comfort and counsel:

> *Many a questioning, many a fear,*
> *Many a doubt, hath its quieting here.*
> *Moment by moment, let down from Heaven,*
> *Time, opportunity, guidance, are given.*
> *Fear not tomorrows, Child of the King,*
> *Trust them with Jesus, DO THE NEXT THING.*
>
> *Do it immediately; do it with prayer;*
> *Do it reliantly, casting all care;*
> *Do it with reverence, tracing His Hand*
> *Who placed it before thee with earnest command.*
> *Stayed on Omnipotence, safe 'neath His wing,*
> *Leave all resultings, DO THE NEXT THING.*[22]

We can do the next thing because we know that God orders the seasons of our lives. Even the most difficult ones. As Romans 8:28 reminds us, "We know that for those who love God all things work together for good, for those who are called according to his purpose." John Piper comments on this verse: "If you live inside this massive promise, your life is as solid as the rock of Gibraltar. Nothing can blow you over inside the walls of Romans 8:28. Outside Romans 8:28 all is confusion and anxiety and fear and uncertainty."[23]

So inside the walls of Romans 8:28, let's take the next step, do the next thing.

Plan to Depend

We hope the simple suggestions in this chapter help you manage the needs and demands of daily life. But let's be clear: this is not a self-help chapter, because if truth be told, we *can't* help ourselves. Whether enduring a trial, contending with an interruption, or enjoying a peaceful day, we must constantly depend upon God's help to be effective daily shoppers of time. No doubt you're nodding your head as we state the obvious.

But what does it mean to depend on God? What does it look like? Proverbs 3:6 answers that question: "In all your ways acknowledge him." Charles Bridges explains how this works out in everyday life:

> Take one step at a time, every step under Divine warrant and direction. Ever plan for yourself in simple dependence on God. It is nothing less than self-idolatry to conceive that we can carry on even the ordinary matters of the day without his counsel. He loves to be consulted.[24]

It's the "ordinary matters of the day" that we often try to accomplish on our own, is it not? When we're faced with a big decision, Proverbs 3:6 is our go-to verse. We're quick to acknowledge our need for God in extraordinary situations. However, it is often in the ordinary matters of our day where our lack of dependence is most evident.

We live for periods of time as if we don't need God in order to clean our bathroom, or to counsel our children, or to make a phone call, or to run that errand. Yet, as Mr. Bridges rightly asserts, this is self-idolatry. We think we're sufficient to handle everyday matters. But, of course, we're not! Rather, we must abandon self-effort and self-idolatry and actively choose to depend on God.

So let's humbly concede that we can't carry out even the most ordinary of activities or meet the simplest of needs apart from God's help. Let's consult God, acknowledging him in all our ways, while not forgetting Mr. Bridges's confident assertion: "He loves to be consulted!"

In the end, our highest goal each day is not flawless execution of our plans or increased productivity. It's our relationship with God, walking in dependence upon him throughout the day. We should not be more consumed with the completion of our to-do list than pleasing and glorifying the Savior. Whether we're sitting down to map out our day, simplifying our to-do list, or receiving an interruption as a "sovereign delivery," we must, above all, plan to depend.

Conclusion

It's another Friday girls' lunch at Mom's kitchen table. This time we're enjoying our second-favorite menu option (after Greek with extra feta): ham and cheese rolls and cinnamon pretzels, hot out of the oven from the Amish market.

We're wrapping up our shopping-for-time discussion, for this book anyway. In reality, though, it's a conversation that never ends. Hardly a week goes by when we don't talk about time's best deals, getting Mom's advice on which bargains to buy up and which to leave for another day. Time is a gift—like the fifty dollars Dad gives us on Outlet Day II—except infinitely more precious. How to make the most of that gift is never far from our minds or conversation.

We hope this modest little volume has inspired you to treasure time as well, to spend it only on the best deals—sitting at Jesus's feet, considering your seasonal priorities, depending on God each and every day. We also hope we've encouraged Kasy, whom we met at the beginning of this book, and all those like her who are exhausted, miserable, and overwhelmed.

But before we conclude, we have one more thought for Kasy. It may just be the most important shopping-for-time advice of all.

Dear Kasy,

You may not have expected such a long reply to your e-mail. But we trust you've enjoyed our shopping-for-time excursion all the same. More than a fun read, we hope we've supplied handles to help you climb out of the overwhelmed and miserable quagmire. Do you see now? Life really doesn't have to be this way! By becoming an effective shopper of time—peace, productivity, and fruitfulness can be normal instead.

You're seventeen, at the threshold of womanhood. God willing, you have many seasons of life ahead of you—seasons that, because they are ordered by the loving Savior, should fill you with joyful expectation. By honing your shopping-for-time skills, you can reap more benefit from each successive season. And when you are seventy-seven you can look back with gratefulness and satisfaction at a life carefully lived. You can testify that it really is possible to do it all and not be overwhelmed. But shopping for time is about more than merely not being overwhelmed.

Kasy, there are a million time-management techniques out there. There are books and tools and seminars and programs and promises. Most of them are more imaginative and effective than any time-saving tip we could offer. And many of them can be helpful in making the best use of our time. But none of them, on its own, will buy us a moment's true peace. They may supply temporary relief, but in the end they can't provide a cure. That's because our biggest problem isn't that we're overwhelmed, miserable, and exhausted. It's that we are sinners, utterly incapable of pleasing a holy God and justly deserving of his wrath—no matter how well we spend our time.

That's the bad news. But, oh, how good is the good news! We trust you know it already, but don't let that keep you from marveling at it once again. This holy God, whom we have offended, does not treat us as our sins deserve. Instead, he sent his Son, Jesus, to earth to die a horrific death on a shameful cross for the likes of us. There our Savior solved our biggest problem: He died to save us from our sins. He absorbed the wrath of God that we deserved. And now, by his substitutionary sacrifice, we have been forgiven for our transgressions, reconciled to God, and clothed in Christ's righteousness.

In light of this wondrous gospel, the following exhortation from Philippians 1:27 is truly amazing. Here we are told to "let your manner of life be worthy of the gospel of Christ." Isn't it mind-boggling, Kasy, to consider that we who were once condemned sinners can now, by the grace of God, live a life worthy of the gospel?

Consider, then, the staggering implications of our shopping-for-time tips. We don't evaluate our priorities, consider relationships, and simplify tasks merely to avoid being overwhelmed. We do it so that our manner of life would be worthy of the gospel. We do it because, by God's amazing grace, we can live a life worthy of the gospel.

But there's more. Not only does the gospel transform our perspective of time on earth, it has eternal implications as well. For one day we will stand before the Lord. Each of us will give an account and be rewarded for how we have used our time in response to his grace. Mercifully, we will not be judged for our sins—those have been covered by our Lord's blood—but we will be evaluated for how we lived our lives for his purposes. And we can look forward to a future reward that we did not earn or deserve, but which God will grant us for walking carefully, all because of his Son.

What a moment that will be. And it will be here before too long. We have a few short years in this present life to determine what will transpire on that day. How we live now affects whether, and to what degree, we will receive the undeserved rewards God so eagerly desires to give us. That's why Matthew Henry wisely counseled us, "It ought to be the business of every day to prepare for our last day."[25]

Kasy, it's our prayer that this book will help you become a wise shopper of time in every season of your life, so when you pass from time into eternity, you can know the intense and indescribable joy of our Savior's pleasure and commendation. We look forward to meeting you there and hearing how God, by his grace, helped you to make the best use of your time here on earth.

Your fellow time shoppers,
Carolyn, Nicole, Kristin, and Janelle

Notes

1. Elisabeth Elliot, "Restlessness and Worry," *The Elisabeth Elliot Newsletter*, September/October 2003 (Ann Arbor, MI: Servant Ministries).

2. John Piper, *When I Don't Desire God* (Wheaton, IL: Crossway, 2004), 116.

3. Martha Peace, *Becoming a Titus 2 Woman* (Bemidji, MN: Focus, 1997), 116–17.

4. C. S. Lewis, *Mere Christianity* (San Francisco: Harper, 2001), 198.

5. You can find an online version of this plan at www.esv.org.

6. We are indebted to Mike Bullmore for this idea.

7. Donald Whitney, *Spiritual Disciplines for the Christian Life* (Colorado Springs: NavPress, 1991).

8. John Piper, *When I Don't Desire God* (Wheaton, IL: Crossway, 2004).

9. Donald Whitney, *Simplify Your Spiritual Life* (Colorado Springs: NavPress, 2003), 157.

10. B. B. Warfield, *The Works of Benjamin B. Warfield* (Grand Rapids, MI: Baker, 1931; repr., 1991), 7:113.

11. Charles Spurgeon, *Morning and Evening* (Peabody, MA: Hendrickson, 1995), 49.

12. Jean Fleming, "Personal Retreat: A Special Date with God," *Discipleship Journal* (http://www.navpress.com/epubs/displayarticle/1/1.60.4.html).

13. Carolyn Mahaney, *Feminine Appeal* (Wheaton, IL: Crossway, 2004).

14. Carolyn Mahaney and Nicole Mahaney Whitacre, *Girl Talk* (Wheaton, IL: Crossway, 2005).

15. Joshua Harris, *I Kissed Dating Goodbye* (Sisters, OR: Multnomah, 2003).

16. Joshua Harris, *Boy Meets Girl* (Sisters, OR: Multnomah, 2005).

17. Joshua Harris, *Sex Is Not the Problem (Lust Is)* (Sisters, OR: Multnomah, 2005).

18. James W. Botkin, "Smart Business: How Knowledge Communities Can Revolutionize Your Company," in Stephanie Winston, *Organized for Success* (New York: Crown Business, 2004), 121–22.

19. Alexander MacLaren in Mary Wilder Tileston, "Joy and Strength" (http://www.backtothebible.org).

20. Elizabeth George, *Life Management for Busy Women* (Eugene, OR: Harvest, 2002), 115–16.

21. "The Letters of C. S. Lewis to Arthur Greeves, 20 December 1943," in *The Quotable Lewis* (Wheaton, IL: Tyndale, 1989), 335.

22. Author unknown.

23. John Piper, "Called According to His Purpose," audio message, October 13, 1985 (http://www.desiringgod.org/ResourceLibrary/Sermons).

24. Charles Bridges, *A Commentary on Proverbs* (Carlisle, PA: Banner of Truth, 1846; repr. 1998), 24.

25. Matthew Henry, *Experiencing God's Presence* (New Kensington, PA: Whitaker, 2002), 169.